The Watts
Picture Atlas

WRITTEN BY SHIRLEY WILLIS

ILLUSTRATED BY NICK HEWETSON

CREATED AND DESIGNED BY DAVID SALARIYA

W

FRANKLIN WATTS

A Division of Scholastic Inc.

NEW YORK • TORONTO • LONDON • AUCKLAND • SYDNEY
MEXICO CITY • NEW DELHI • HONG KONG
DANBURY, CONNECTICUT

Contents

THE ARCTIC 60

CANADA AND
GREENLAND
10-11

UNITED STATES:
THE WEST AND
MIDWEST 12-13

U.S.: THE MIDWEST
AND NORTHEAST
14-15

U.S.: THE SOUTH
16-17

MEXICO, CENTRAL
AMERICA, AND THE
CARIBBEAN 18-19

SOUTH AMERICA 20-21

The Earth in Space	4
How the World Becomes a Flat Map	6
How the Pages Work in This Atlas	8
Canada and Greenland	10
United States: The West and Midwest	12
United States: The Midwest and Northeast	14
United States: The South	16
Mexico, Central America, and the Caribbean	18
South America	20
Scandinavia, Finland, and Iceland	22
The British Isles	24
Spain and Portugal	26
France	28
Belgium, Netherlands, and Luxembourg	30
Germany, Austria, and Switzerland	32
Italy and Malta	34
Greece and the Greek Islands	36
Central and Eastern Europe	38
Northern Eurasia	40
Southwest Asia	42
Northern Africa	44
Southern Africa	46
India and Its Neighbors	48
Japan	50
Southeast Asia	52
China, Mongolia, Korea, and Taiwan	54
Australia and Papua New Guinea	56
New Zealand	58
Southwestern Pacific Islands	59
The Arctic	60
The Antarctic	61
Glossary and Index	62

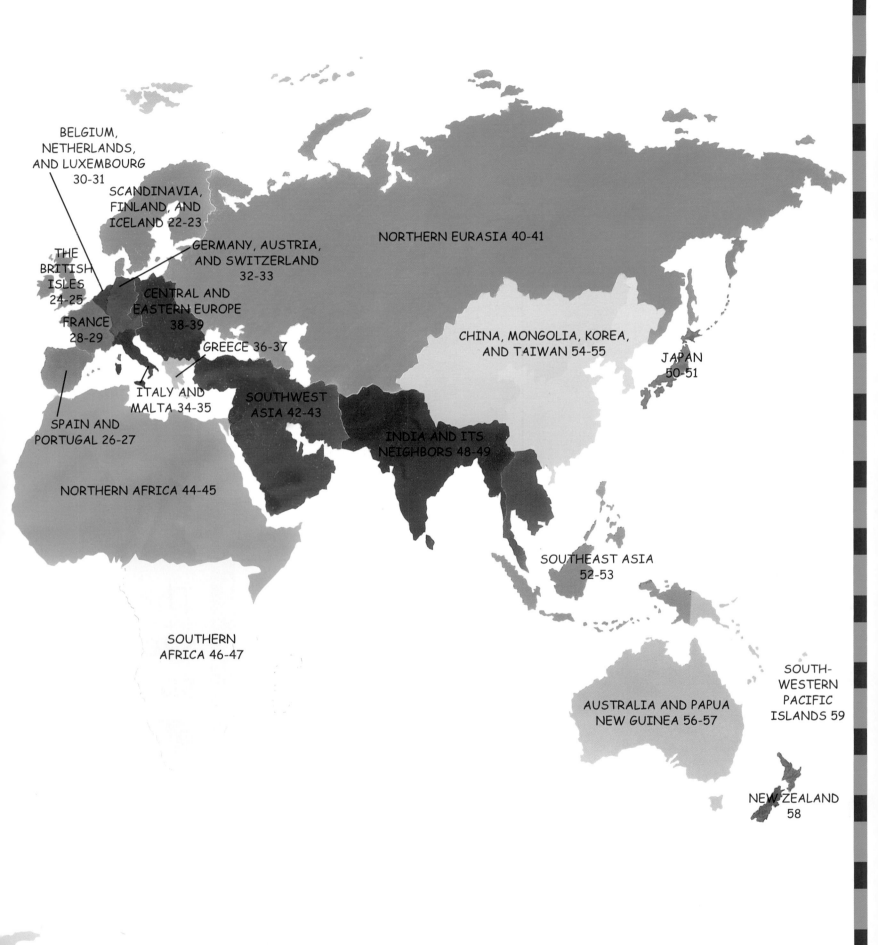

BELGIUM,
NETHERLANDS,
AND LUXEMBOURG
30-31

SCANDINAVIA,
FINLAND, AND
ICELAND 22-23

GERMANY, AUSTRIA,
AND SWITZERLAND
32-33

THE
BRITISH
ISLES
24-25

CENTRAL AND
EASTERN EUROPE
38-39

FRANCE
28-29

GREECE 36-37

ITALY AND
MALTA 34-35

SPAIN AND
PORTUGAL 26-27

SOUTHWEST
ASIA 42-43

NORTHERN AFRICA 44-45

INDIA AND ITS
NEIGHBORS 48-49

NORTHERN EURASIA 40-41

CHINA, MONGOLIA, KOREA,
AND TAIWAN 54-55

JAPAN
50-51

SOUTHERN
AFRICA 46-47

SOUTHEAST ASIA
52-53

AUSTRALIA AND PAPUA
NEW GUINEA 56-57

SOUTH-
WESTERN
PACIFIC
ISLANDS 59

NEW ZEALAND
58

THE ANTARCTIC 61

3

The Earth in Space

The Earth is a ball of rock
that orbits the Sun.
It uses the Sun's energy
for warmth and light.

The Earth is one of nine
planets that orbit (circle) the
Sun. Together they form the
Solar System. Each planet
orbits the Sun in an elliptical
(oval) path. The length of a
planet's orbit depends on its
distance from the Sun. Mercury
is closest and takes eighty-
eight days to orbit the Sun.
Pluto's orbit takes 250 years
because it is the outermost
planet in the Solar System.
The Earth's orbit takes about
365 days.

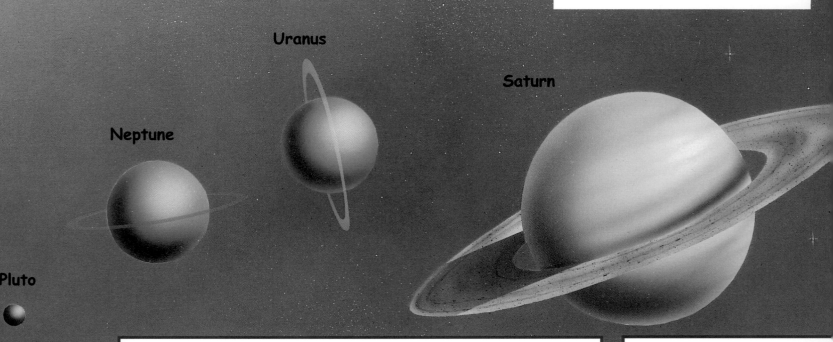

Uranus

Neptune

Saturn

Pluto

The Earth is always
moving. As it orbits
the Sun, the planet
spins on its axis,
making one complete
turn every 24 hours.
As one side of its
surface is lit by the
Sun, the other side is
in darkness. This is
why we have daytime
and nighttime.

The Earth's axis is
an imaginary line
running through
its center.

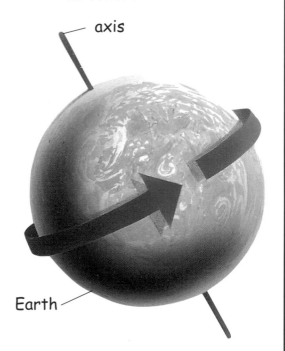

axis

Earth

The Earth seen from space

The Earth is 93 million miles (148,800,000 km) from the Sun. It is neither too hot nor too cold. Earth is the only planet in the Solar System where life is known to exist.

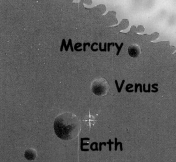

Mercury

Venus

Earth

Mars

Sun

Jupiter

From space, the Earth is seen as a huge round ball. The planet looks blue because much of its surface is covered in oceans. Large land masses, called continents, can also be seen. Closer up, the Earth looks flat. From an airplane, the towns, roads, rivers, and railroad tracks below divide the countryside into a huge patchwork pattern. People are too small to be seen from this distance. If you look down from a skyscraper, people below can be seen, but they look as small as ants. Cars on the street look like toys.

The Earth seen from an airplane

The Earth seen from a tall building

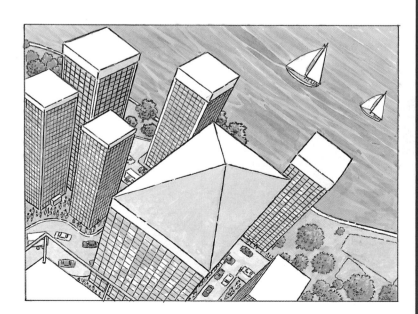

How the World Becomes a Flat Map

A globe is a round map of the world. Mapmakers make a flat map of the world for an atlas.

Our planet is made up of four layers (below). The surface of the Earth, where we live, is called the crust. Every continent and ocean lies on the Earth's crust. Beneath the crust is a layer of rock called the mantle. Parts of the mantle are hot and molten (liquid) and can break through the crust to form a volcano. The core of the planet has two parts. The outer core is hot, molten metal. The inner core is solid metal.

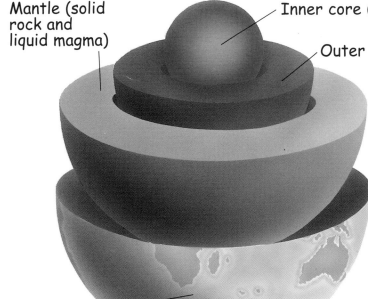

Mantle (solid rock and liquid magma)

Inner core (solid metal)

Outer core (liquid)

Crust

Mapmakers divide the world's surface into segments. They are laid side by side like the skin of an orange, but this leaves gaps in the map (above). Then parts of the world are "stretched" so that the map becomes whole. This process is called map projection. On the flat maps in an atlas, the countries are shaped slightly differently than they are on a globe.

Mapmakers use a grid of imaginary lines across the globe to help plot the exact positions of places. Lines of longitude are drawn from north to south, and lines of latitude go from east to west.

The equator is an imaginary line dividing the world in half. It is positioned at latitude 0° (zero degrees). The northern hemisphere is above the equator, and the southern hemisphere is below it.

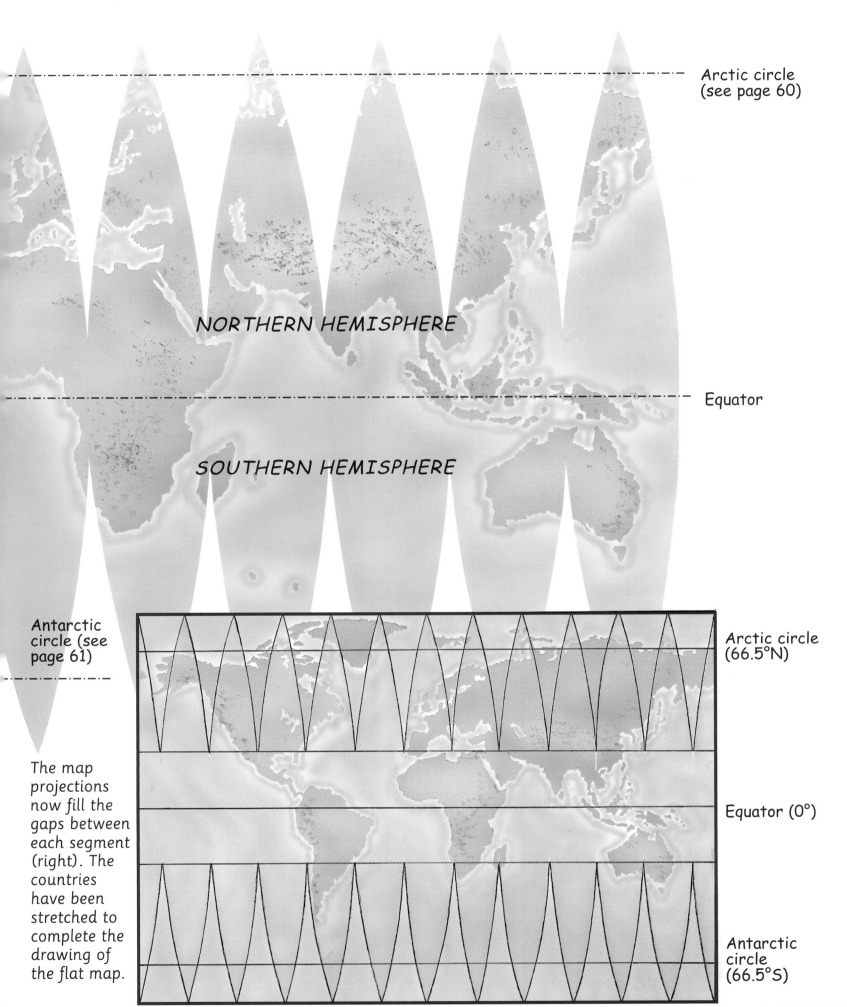

Arctic circle (see page 60)

NORTHERN HEMISPHERE

Equator

SOUTHERN HEMISPHERE

Antarctic circle (see page 61)

The map projections now fill the gaps between each segment (right). The countries have been stretched to complete the drawing of the flat map.

Arctic circle (66.5°N)

Equator (0°)

Antarctic circle (66.5°S)

How the Pages Work in This Atlas

Here is the kind of map you will find in this atlas. Each page shows a map of different countries of the world. The notes on this page explain the type of information given on each map.

Look on the map for buildings or other places of interest that are shown in the "Can you find..." box.

A large, bold label in capital letters shows a country name.

A thick dotted line shows the border between countries. (A thin dotted line shows the border of states within a country.)

The globe shows where the countries on each map are in the world.

A small label like this shows the name of a lake or river.

A curved label like this shows the name of a sea or ocean.

Go to the fact box for extra information about each country or continent.

Scandinavia, F and Iceland

Norway, Sweden, and Denmark are known as Scandinavia. These countries are rich in natural resources such as timber, fish, oil, and natural gas. They have warm summers and bitterly cold winters.

Can you find...
a stave church?

Legoland?

oil rig

stave church

skiing

NORWAY

Bergen

fishing boat

ski jumping

SW

Nor spru

Drottningholm Palace

OSLO

SCANDINAVIA, FINLAND, AND ICELAND

L. Vänern

L. Vättern

Gothenburg

Little Mermaid

Legoland

Kalmar Castle

NORTH SEA

DENMARK

COPENHAGEN

BAL

GERMANY

NORWEG SEA

Fact:
Hammerfest in Norway is the most northerly town in the world.

Maps like this show a faraway country and its position near the region of the main map.

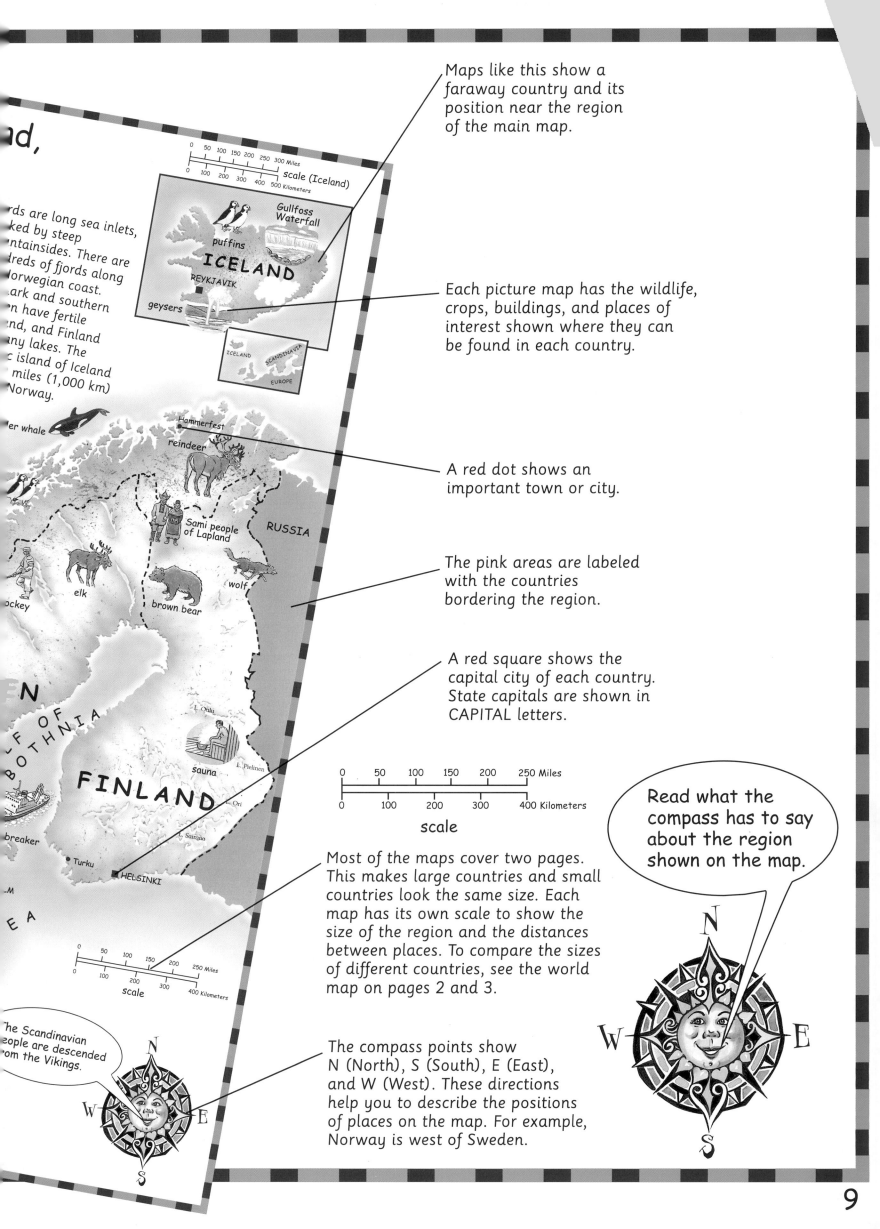

scale (Iceland)
0   50 100 150 200 250 300 Miles
0   100 200 300 400 500 Kilometers

Gullfoss Waterfall

puffins

ICELAND

REYKJAVIK

geysers

ICELAND

SCANDINAVIA

EUROPE

Each picture map has the wildlife, crops, buildings, and places of interest shown where they can be found in each country.

...rds are long sea inlets,
...ked by steep
...ntainsides. There are
...dreds of fjords along
...lorwegian coast.
...ark and southern
...n have fertile
...nd, and Finland
...any lakes. The
...c island of Iceland
... miles (1,000 km)
...Norway.

...er whale

Hammerfest

reindeer

Sami people of Lapland

RUSSIA

puffins

elk

brown bear

wolf

...ckey

A red dot shows an important town or city.

The pink areas are labeled with the countries bordering the region.

N

...F OF
...OTHNIA

L. Oulu

sauna

L. Pielinen

FINLAND

... Ori

Saimaa

...breaker

Turku

HELSINKI

...-M

E A

A red square shows the capital city of each country. State capitals are shown in CAPITAL letters.

scale
0   50   100   150   200   250 Miles
0   100   200   300   400 Kilometers

Read what the compass has to say about the region shown on the map.

Most of the maps cover two pages. This makes large countries and small countries look the same size. Each map has its own scale to show the size of the region and the distances between places. To compare the sizes of different countries, see the world map on pages 2 and 3.

scale
0   50   100   150   200   250 Miles
0   100   200   300   400 Kilometers

The Scandinavian ...eople are descended ...om the Vikings.

N

W   E

S

The compass points show N (North), S (South), E (East), and W (West). These directions help you to describe the positions of places on the map. For example, Norway is west of Sweden.

N

W   E

S

Canada and Greenland

Canada is the second-biggest country in the world, but it does not have a large population. Few people live in northern Canada because the climate there is too harsh.

Canada has two official languages: English and French. Montreal (above), in Quebec, is the largest French-speaking city in the world after Paris.

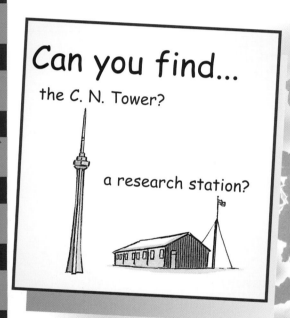

Can you find...

the C. N. Tower?

a research station?

There are high, rocky mountain ranges in the west and rich, flat farmlands called "the prairies" in the central area of Canada. Most Canadians live in the big cities in the southeast, where the climate is milder.

Greenland is the largest island in the world. It belongs to Denmark but has its own government. The Inuit, who live in northern Canada and Greenland, still hunt seals and polar bears.

ARCTIC OCEAN

polar bear

ice-breaker

PACIFIC OCEAN

ALASKA (U.S.)

CANADA

Mackenzie R.

Great Bear L.

NUNAVUT

YUKON TERRITORY

NORTHWEST TERRITORIES

WHITEHORSE

YELLOWKNIFE

moose

Great Slave L.

Douglas fir tree

BRITISH COLUMBIA

SASKATCH-

ROCKY MOUNTAINS

ALBERTA

EDMONTON

Columbia R.

grizzly bear

REGINA

VICTORIA

Vancouver

UNITED STATES

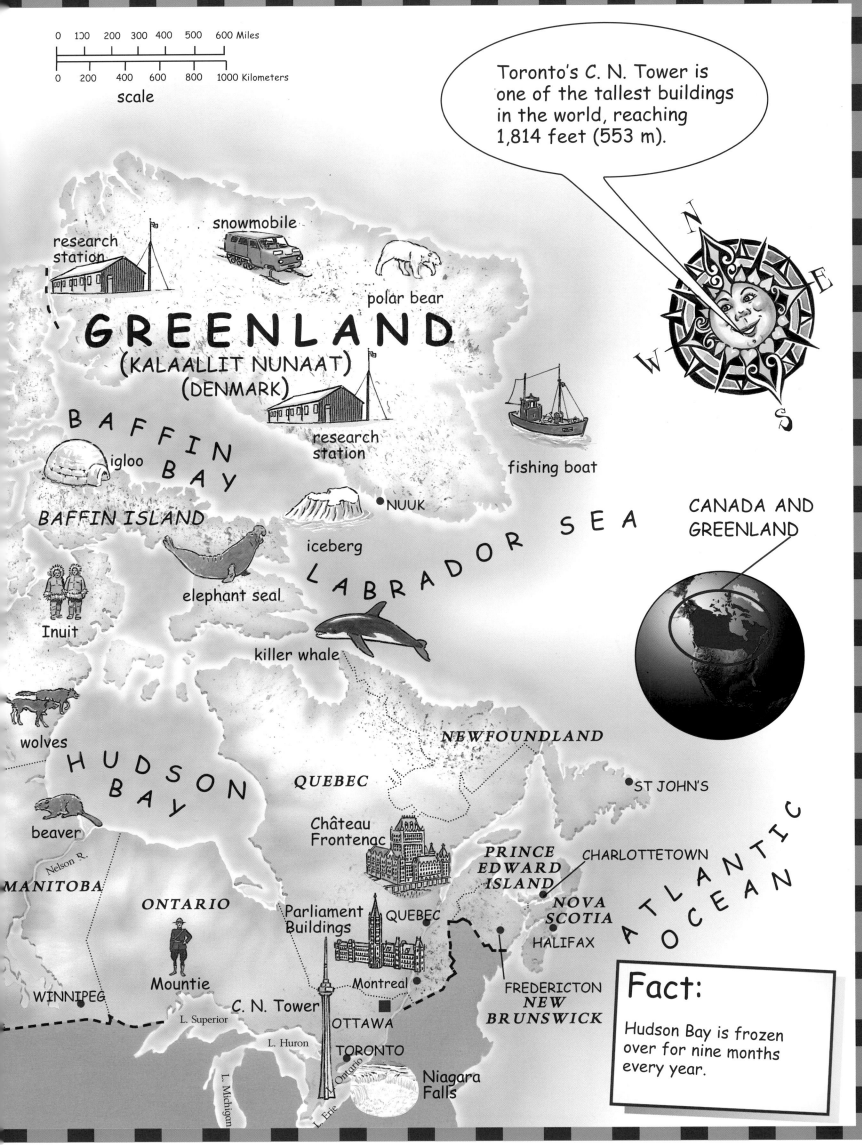

scale

0 100 200 300 400 500 600 Miles

0 200 400 600 800 1000 Kilometers

Toronto's C. N. Tower is one of the tallest buildings in the world, reaching 1,814 feet (553 m).

research station

snowmobile

polar bear

GREENLAND
(KALAALLIT NUNAAT)
(DENMARK)

research station

fishing boat

BAFFIN BAY

igloo

BAFFIN ISLAND

NUUK

iceberg

elephant seal

LABRADOR SEA

CANADA AND GREENLAND

Inuit

killer whale

wolves

NEWFOUNDLAND

HUDSON BAY

QUEBEC

ST JOHN'S

beaver

Château Frontenac

Nelson R.

MANITOBA

ONTARIO

Parliament Buildings

QUEBEC

PRINCE EDWARD ISLAND

CHARLOTTETOWN

NOVA SCOTIA

ATLANTIC OCEAN

Mountie

HALIFAX

WINNIPEG

C. N. Tower

Montreal

L. Superior

OTTAWA

FREDERICTON
NEW BRUNSWICK

L. Huron

TORONTO

L. Michigan

L. Ontario

L. Erie

Niagara Falls

Fact:

Hudson Bay is frozen over for nine months every year.

United States: The West and Midwest

The United States is one of the wealthiest countries in the world. It is made up of fifty states. The western states include Alaska in the far north and Hawaii, 2,485 miles (4,000 km) out in the Pacific Ocean.

The rugged landscape of the West is dominated by the Rocky Mountains. California is the largest state in the region. More people live there than in any other state.

PACIFIC OCEAN

Seattle
OLYMPIA
WASHINGTON

Columbia R.

Portland
SALEM

OREGON

redwood tree

BOISE

Golden Gate Bridge

NEVADA

Reno
CARSON CITY

SACRAMENTO

San Francisco

wild horses

CALIFORNIA

grey whale

Las Vegas • L. Mead

HOLLYWOOD

Los Angeles

San Diego

Colorado R.

scale

0   100   200   300 Miles
0   100   200   300   400   500 Kilometers

PACIFIC OCEAN

caribou
ALASKA

walrus

Anchorage

whale

JUNEAU

0   200   400   600 Miles
0   200 400 600 800 1000 Kilometers
scale (Alaska)

ALASKA

UNITED STATES

N
W   E
S

Hamburgers were invented in the United States and are now eaten all over the world.

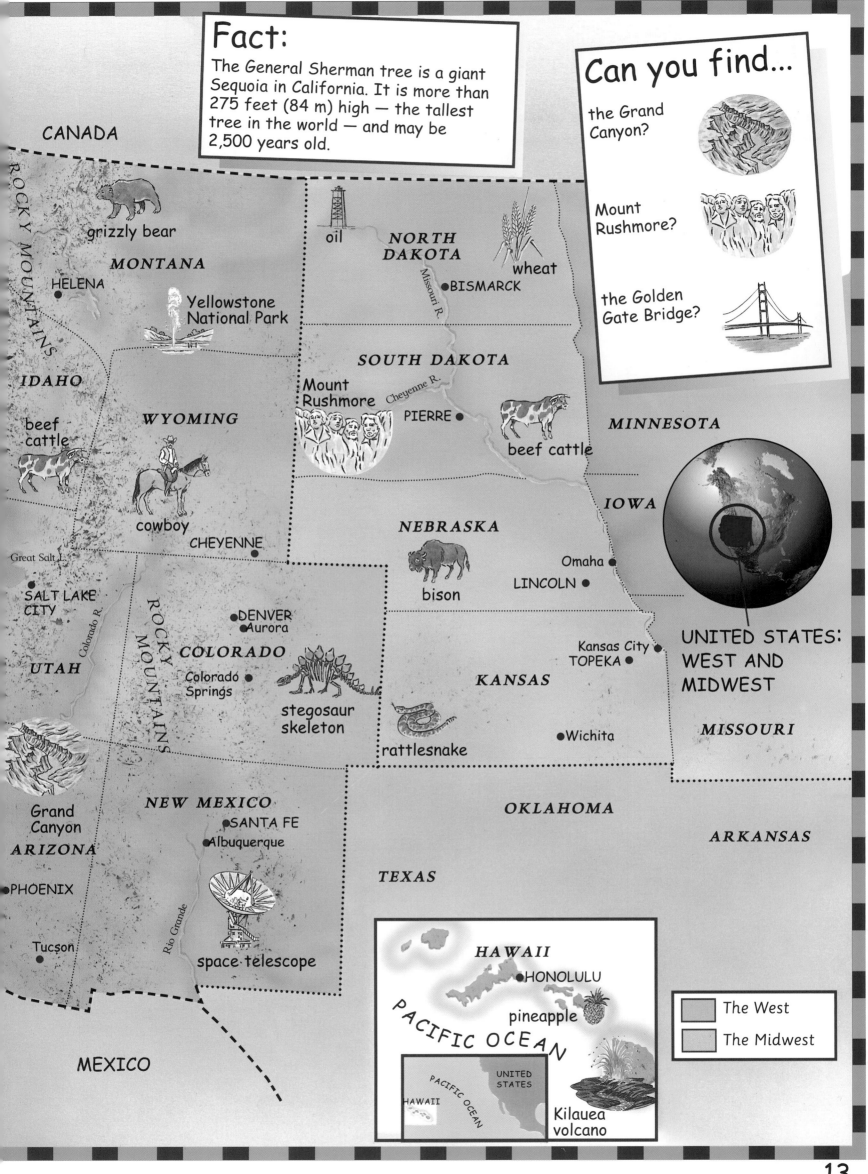

Fact:
The General Sherman tree is a giant Sequoia in California. It is more than 275 feet (84 m) high — the tallest tree in the world — and may be 2,500 years old.

Can you find...
the Grand Canyon?

Mount Rushmore?

the Golden Gate Bridge?

CANADA

ROCKY MOUNTAINS

grizzly bear

MONTANA

HELENA

Yellowstone National Park

oil

NORTH DAKOTA

Missouri R.

wheat

BISMARCK

IDAHO

SOUTH DAKOTA

Mount Rushmore

Cheyenne R.

PIERRE

beef cattle

MINNESOTA

beef cattle

WYOMING

cowboy

CHEYENNE

Great Salt L.

SALT LAKE CITY

NEBRASKA

bison

Omaha

LINCOLN

IOWA

UNITED STATES: WEST AND MIDWEST

Colorado R.

ROCKY MOUNTAINS

DENVER
Aurora

COLORADO

Colorado Springs

stegosaur skeleton

UTAH

KANSAS

Kansas City
TOPEKA

Wichita

MISSOURI

rattlesnake

Grand Canyon

NEW MEXICO

SANTA FE

Albuquerque

OKLAHOMA

ARKANSAS

ARIZONA

PHOENIX

Rio Grande

TEXAS

space telescope

Tucson

HAWAII

HONOLULU

pineapple

PACIFIC OCEAN

PACIFIC OCEAN

UNITED STATES

HAWAII

Kilauea volcano

MEXICO

	The West
	The Midwest

United States: The Midwest and Northeast

The United States is the world's most industrial country. The area around the Great Lakes supplies most of the nation's iron and steel. Detroit is the center of the American car industry.

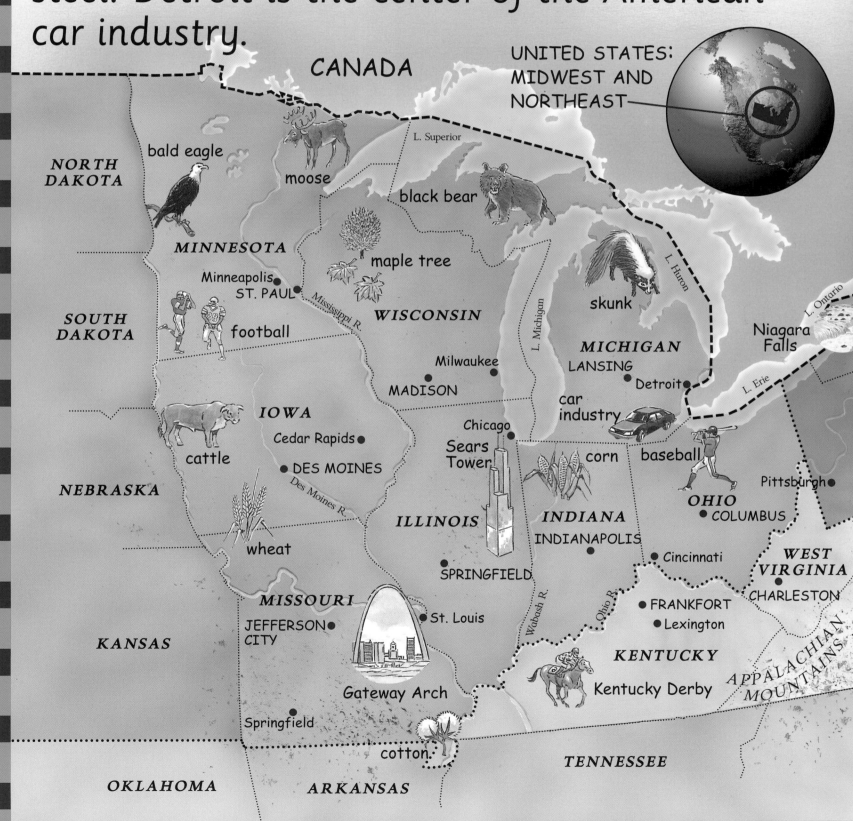

UNITED STATES: MIDWEST AND NORTHEAST

CANADA

L. Superior

bald eagle

NORTH DAKOTA

moose

black bear

MINNESOTA

maple tree

Minneapolis
ST. PAUL

SOUTH DAKOTA

football

Mississippi R.

WISCONSIN

L. Michigan

skunk

L. Huron

MICHIGAN

LANSING

Detroit

L. Erie

L. Ontario

Niagara Falls

Milwaukee

MADISON

cattle

IOWA

Cedar Rapids

DES MOINES

Des Moines R.

NEBRASKA

wheat

ILLINOIS

Chicago

Sears Tower

car industry

corn

baseball

Pittsburgh

OHIO

COLUMBUS

INDIANA

INDIANAPOLIS

Cincinnati

WEST VIRGINIA

CHARLESTON

SPRINGFIELD

Wabash R.

Ohio R.

FRANKFORT

Lexington

MISSOURI

JEFFERSON CITY

St. Louis

KANSAS

Gateway Arch

KENTUCKY

Kentucky Derby

APPALACHIAN MOUNTAINS

Springfield

cotton

TENNESSEE

OKLAHOMA

ARKANSAS

Can you find...

the Sears Tower?

the Statue of Liberty?

the Gateway Arch?

The flat, fertile plains of the Midwestern states produce so much wheat and corn that the area is known as the "breadbasket of the world." Over the Appalachian Mountains lie the great cities of the Atlantic coast. New York City is the largest city in the United States, with a population of sixteen million.

Fact:

The White House in Washington, D.C., has been the home of U.S. presidents for nearly two hundred years.

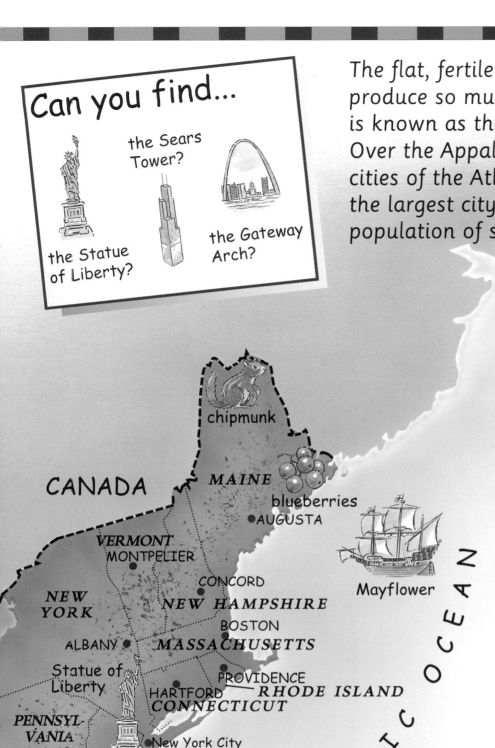

CANADA

chipmunk

MAINE

blueberries
AUGUSTA

Mayflower

VERMONT
MONTPELIER

CONCORD

NEW YORK

NEW HAMPSHIRE

BOSTON

ALBANY

MASSACHUSETTS

Statue of Liberty

PROVIDENCE

HARTFORD

RHODE ISLAND

CONNECTICUT

PENNSYL-VANIA

New York City

HARRISBURG

TRENTON

Philadelphia

NEW JERSEY

DOVER

DELAWARE

ANNAPOLIS

MARYLAND

WASHINGTON, D.C.

RICHMOND

Norfolk

VIRGINIA

NORTH CAROLINA

ATLANTIC OCEAN

Minke whale

Note: These light green states are part of the South (see pages 16 and 17).

The Statue of Liberty was built by Gustav Eiffel in Paris, France. It was shipped to the United States in pieces and put together there. A staircase inside its hollow structure allows visitors to climb up to Liberty's crown.

Rhode Island is the smallest state in the United States.

The Midwest
The Northeast

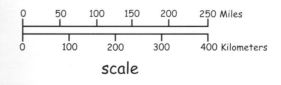
0 50 100 150 200 250 Miles

0 100 200 300 400 Kilometers

scale

15

United States: The South

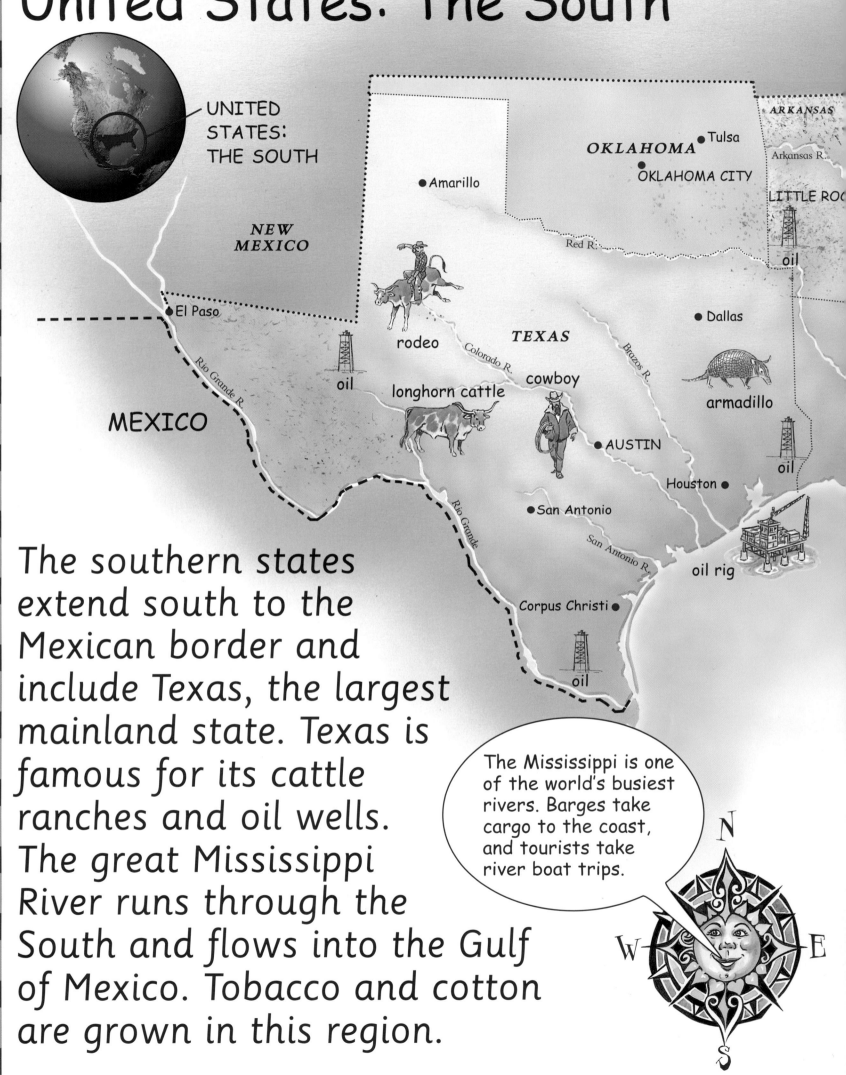

UNITED STATES: THE SOUTH

ARKANSAS

OKLAHOMA • Tulsa

Arkansas R.

OKLAHOMA CITY

LITTLE ROC

• Amarillo

NEW MEXICO

oil

Red R.

El Paso

rodeo

Colorado R.

TEXAS

cowboy

Brazos R.

• Dallas

armadillo

oil

Rio Grande R.

oil

longhorn cattle

MEXICO

• AUSTIN

Houston •

Rio Grande

• San Antonio

San Antonio R.

oil rig

Corpus Christi •

oil

The southern states extend south to the Mexican border and include Texas, the largest mainland state. Texas is famous for its cattle ranches and oil wells. The great Mississippi River runs through the South and flows into the Gulf of Mexico. Tobacco and cotton are grown in this region.

The Mississippi is one of the world's busiest rivers. Barges take cargo to the coast, and tourists take river boat trips.

N
W   E
S

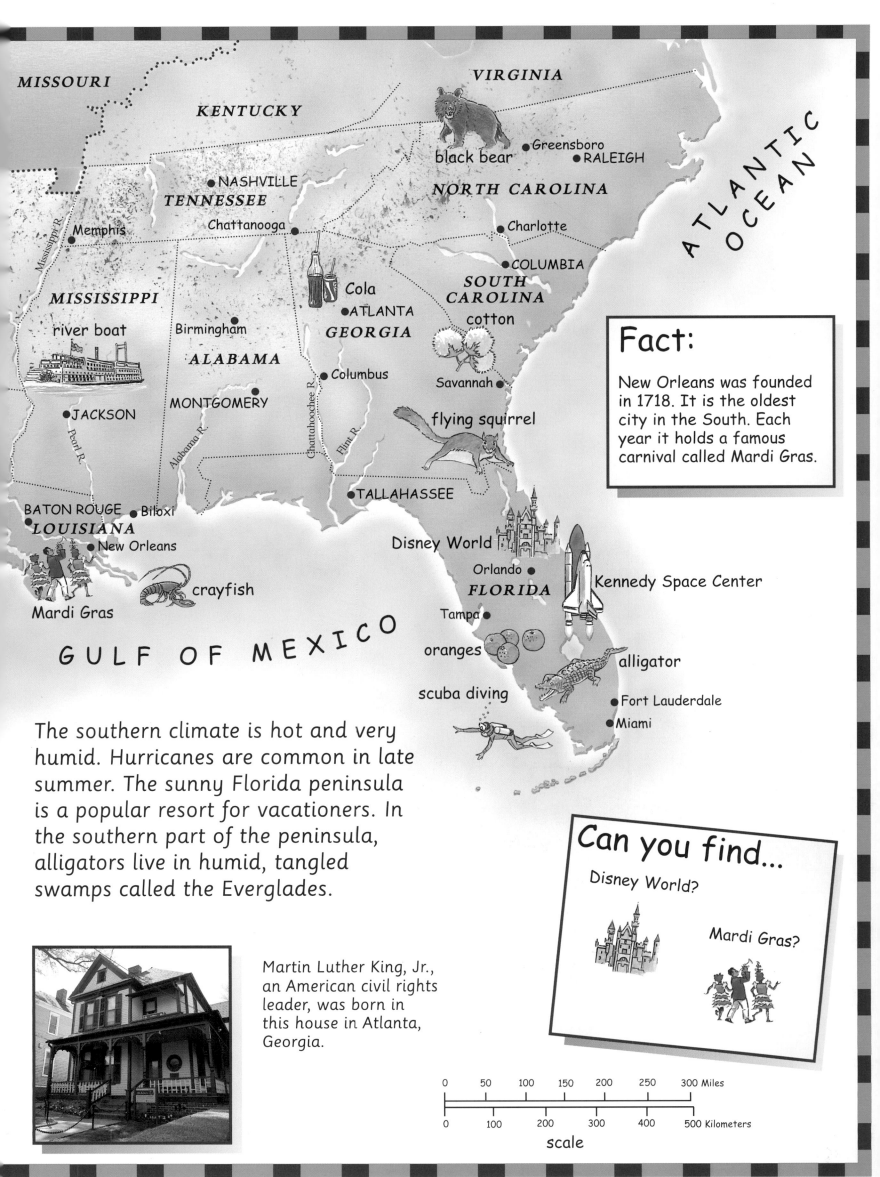

MISSOURI

KENTUCKY

VIRGINIA

black bear

Greensboro
● RALEIGH

● NASHVILLE

TENNESSEE

NORTH CAROLINA

Memphis

Chattanooga

● Charlotte

Mississippi R.

MISSISSIPPI

river boat

Birmingham

Cola

ALABAMA

● ATLANTA

GEORGIA

● COLUMBIA

SOUTH
CAROLINA

cotton

● Columbus

Chattahoochee R.

Savannah ●

Flint R.

flying squirrel

● JACKSON

MONTGOMERY

Alabama R.

Pearl R.

● TALLAHASSEE

BATON ROUGE

● Biloxi

LOUISIANA

● New Orleans

Disney World

crayfish

Mardi Gras

Orlando ●

FLORIDA

Kennedy Space Center

GULF OF MEXICO

Tampa ●

oranges

alligator

scuba diving

● Fort Lauderdale

● Miami

ATLANTIC OCEAN

Fact:

New Orleans was founded in 1718. It is the oldest city in the South. Each year it holds a famous carnival called Mardi Gras.

The southern climate is hot and very humid. Hurricanes are common in late summer. The sunny Florida peninsula is a popular resort for vacationers. In the southern part of the peninsula, alligators live in humid, tangled swamps called the Everglades.

Martin Luther King, Jr., an American civil rights leader, was born in this house in Atlanta, Georgia.

Can you find...

Disney World?

Mardi Gras?

0	50	100	150	200	250	300 Miles

0	100	200	300	400	500 Kilometers

scale

Mexico, Central America, and the Caribbean

MEXICO, CENTRAL AMERICA, AND THE CARIBBEAN

UNITED STATES

seal

cactus

vampire bat

cotton

cotton

leatherback turtle

great white shark

PACIFIC OCEAN

MEXICO

GULF OF MEXICO

gold

corn

National Cathedral

oil rig

MEXICO CITY

Olmec stone heads

Acapulco

dolphin

Mexico and Central America link the continents of North and South America. The land is mountainous, and much of it is covered by tropical rain forests. The Panama Canal, in the south of the region, provides a link for ships between the Atlantic and Pacific Oceans.

Can you find...

Chichén Itzá?

the Olmec stone heads?

the National Cathedral?

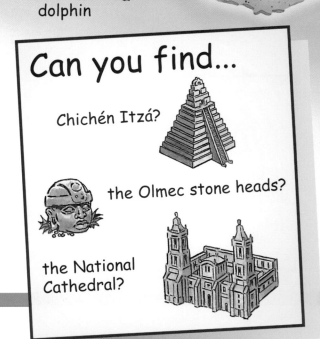

18

Mexico is this region's largest country. It is rich in silver and oil. Bananas and coffee grow in Central America and the Caribbean. The warm seas and climate of the Caribbean's volcanic islands attract many tourists.

This region is a hurricane zone. Fierce tropical storms sweep the Gulf of Mexico, and the enormous waves they create cause a lot of damage.

CARIBBEAN ISLANDS

PUERTO RICO (U.S.)
SAN JUAN
BRITISH VIRGIN ISLANDS
ROAD TOWN
THE VALLEY
(UK)
ANGUILLA (UK)
VIRGIN ISLANDS (U.S.)
BASSETERRE
ANTIGUA AND BARBUDA
ST. JOHNS
ST. KITTS AND NEVIS
PLYMOUTH
GUADELOUPE (FRANCE)
MONTSERRAT (UK)
BASSE-TERRE
DOMINICA
ROSEAU
FORT-DE-FRANCE
MARTINIQUE
CASTRIES
ST. LUCIA
ST. VINCENT AND THE GRENADINES
BARBADOS
GRENADA
ST. GEORGE'S
BRIDGETOWN
TRINIDAD AND TOBAGO
PORT OF SPAIN

ATLANTIC OCEAN
CARIBBEAN ISLANDS
SOUTH AMERICA

0 100 200 300 Miles
0 100 200 300 400 500 Kilometers
scale

tobacco

NASSAU
BAHAMAS

scuba diving

HAVANA
CUBA

DOMINICAN REPUBLIC

Chichén Itzá

Cancún

PORT-AU-PRINCE
SANTO DOMINGO

cricket
HAITI

oil rig

C A R I B B E A N   S E A

JAMAICA
KINGSTON

BELMOPAN
BELIZE

The city of Chichén Itzá was built in the 1100s by the people of the Maya civilization.

GUATEMALA
HONDURAS
GUATEMALA CITY
TEGUCIGALPA

N

SAN SALVADOR
EL SALVADOR
MANAGUA

ray

NICARAGUA

W   E

COSTA RICA
SAN JOSÉ

Panama Canal
PANAMA CITY

coffee
toucan
PANAMA
COLOMBIA

S

South America

Machu Picchu was a holy city, built by the Inca civilization in the 1400s. This ancient mountaintop settlement in the Peruvian Andes was rediscovered in 1911.

SOUTH AMERICA

Tomatoes were first discovered growing in South America.

N
E
W
S

scale

0   100 200 300 400 500 600 Miles
0   200 400 600 800 1000 Kilometers

ATLANTIC OCEAN

CARACAS

Angel Falls

VENEZUELA

green turtle

PANAMA

COLOMBIA
BOGOTÁ

coffee

QUITO

EQUADOR

SOUTH AMERICA

scale (Galapagos Islands)

0   25   30 Miles
0   25   50 Kilometers

GALAPAGOS ISLANDS (ECUADOR)

giant tortoise

marine iguana

GUYANA
GEORGETOWN

Ariane rocket launch site

PARAMARIBO

SURINAME

CAYENNE

FRENCH GUIANA (FRANCE)

piranha

jaguar

tarantula

Machu Picchu

PERU

Ucayali R.

anaconda

Tapajós R.

Xingu R.

Amazon R.

rain forest

BRAZIL

Natal

The Andes Mountains run the length of the huge continent of South America. In the north, the Amazon River runs through vast tropical rain forests full of wildlife. In the south, millions of cattle and sheep are reared on fertile grasslands called the pampas.

South America is rich in oil, silver, copper, coal, and iron ore. The continent's largest country, Brazil, is the world's leading coffee producer. Spanish is spoken throughout South America except in Brazil, where the language is Portuguese.

Can you find...

the Statue of Christ?

Machu Picchu?

Angel Falls?

Sugarloaf Mountain

BRASÍLIA

Brasília Cathedral

Rio de Janeiro

Statue of Christ

ATLANTIC OCEAN

diamond

PARAGUAY

ASUNCIÓN

URUGUAY

MONTEVIDEO

BOLIVIA

LA PAZ

SUCRE

Andean condor

ANDES

llama

BUENOS AIRES

ARGENTINA

SANTIAGO

volcano

cattle

sheep

CHILE

oil

FALKLAND ISLANDS (UK)

STANLEY

oil

21

Scandinavia, Finland, and Iceland

Norway, Sweden, and Denmark are known as Scandinavia. These countries are rich in natural resources such as timber, fish, oil, and natural gas. They have warm summers and bitterly cold winters.

Fjords are long sea inlets, banked by steep mountainsides. There are hundreds of fjords along the Norwegian coast. Denmark and southern Sweden have fertile farmland, and Finland has many lakes. The volcanic island of Iceland lies 620 miles (1,000 km) west of Norway.

scale (Iceland)

0 50 100 150 200 250 300 Miles
0 100 200 300 400 500 Kilometers

Gullfoss Waterfall

ICELAND

REYKJAVIK

puffins

geysers

SCANDINAVIA

EUROPE

ICELAND

RUSSIA

wolf

brown bear

Sami people of Lapland

reindeer

Hammerfest

elk

ice hockey

killer whale

NORWEGIAN SEA

Can you find...

Legoland?

a stave church?

FINLAND

sauna

L. Oulu
L. Pielinen
L. Ori

HELSINKI

Turku

scale

250 Miles
400 Kilometers

The Scandinavian people are descended from the Vikings.

N
E
S
W

SWEDEN

GULF OF BOTHNIA

L. Stor

Norwegian spruce

ice-breaker

Uppsala

STOCKHOLM

Drottningholm Palace

BALTIC SEA

Fact:

Hammerfest in Norway is the most northerly town in the world.

skiing

stave church

ski jumping

OSLO

NORWAY

Bergen

L. Vänern

L. Vättern

Gothenburg

Kalmar Castle

COPENHAGEN

Little Mermaid

Legoland

DENMARK

GERMANY

oil rig

fishing boat

SCANDINAVIA, FINLAND, AND ICELAND

NORTH SEA

23

The British Isles

The United Kingdom (UK) and Ireland are known as the British Isles. Much of the land is farmed, but there are many large cities. London, the biggest city and the capital of the UK, is a major financial and cultural center. The Channel Tunnel links the UK with mainland Europe.

Fact:

The Forth Bridge in Scotland was the first major bridge in the world to be built of steel.

SHETLAND ISLES (UK)

Lerwick

60 Miles

100 Kilometers

30
75

50

25

0
0

scale (Shetland Isles)

IRELAND
UK

Can you find...

the Giant's Causeway?

Edinburgh Castle?

150 Miles

200 Kilometers

100

100

50

50

0
0

scale

oil rig

fishing boat

Highland cattle

Balmoral Castle

red deer

Loch Ness

SCOTLAND

EDINBURGH

Edinburgh Castle

Glasgow

Hadrian's Wall

sheep

Harris tweed

BELFAST

Giant's Causeway

NORTHERN IRELAND

ATLANTIC OCEAN

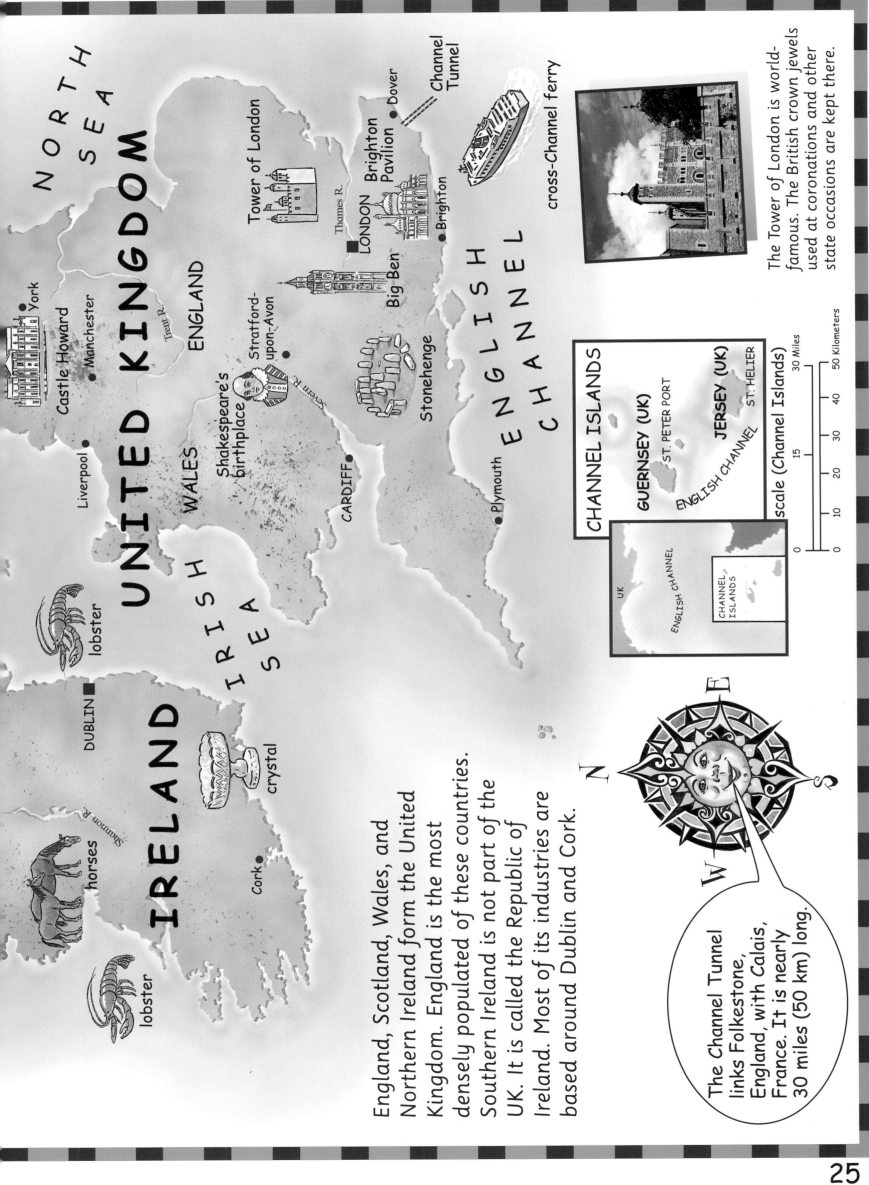

NORTH SEA

UNITED KINGDOM

IRELAND

North Sea

York

Castle Howard

Manchester

Liverpool

Trent R.

ENGLAND

WALES

Shakespeare's birthplace

Stratford-upon-Avon

Severn R.

CARDIFF

Stonehenge

Big Ben

Thames R.

LONDON

Tower of London

Brighton Pavilion

Brighton

Dover

Channel Tunnel

cross-Channel ferry

Plymouth

ENGLISH CHANNEL

IRISH SEA

DUBLIN

Shannon R.

horses

lobster

Cork

crystal

lobster

The Tower of London is world-famous. The British crown jewels used at coronations and other state occasions are kept there.

CHANNEL ISLANDS

GUERNSEY (UK)
ST. PETER PORT

JERSEY (UK)
ST. HELIER

ENGLISH CHANNEL

scale (Channel Islands)

0   10   20   30   40   50 Kilometers
0   15   30 Miles

UK

ENGLISH CHANNEL

CHANNEL ISLANDS

England, Scotland, Wales, and Northern Ireland form the United Kingdom. England is the most densely populated of these countries. Southern Ireland is not part of the UK. It is called the Republic of Ireland. Most of its industries are based around Dublin and Cork.

The Channel Tunnel links Folkestone, England, with Calais, France. It is nearly 30 miles (50 km) long.

N
E
S
W

Spain and Portugal

SPAIN AND PORTUGAL

Madrid is the highest capital city in Europe, at 2,099 feet (640 m) above sea level.

ATLANTIC OCEAN

corn

grapes

• Oporto

PORTUGAL

House of Shells

Tagus R.

■ LISBON

olives

oranges

cork trees

lynx

Seville •
grapes

Rock of Gibraltar

GIBRALTAR (UK)

brown bear

Spain and Portugal form the Iberian Peninsula. They are separated from the rest of Europe by the Pyrenees Mountains. Most of the peninsula is dry grassland with olive groves. This region is dry and hot in summer.

Antonio Gaudi began work on Barcelona's famous church, the Sagrada Familia, in 1883. The construction still continues today.

0   25   50   75   100   125 Miles

0   50   100   150   200 Kilometers

scale

MOROCCO

Can you find...
the Sagrada Familia?

Alhambra Palace?

BAY OF BISCAY

•Bilbao

FRANCE

cave paintings (Altamira)

running with the bulls

PYRENEES

skiing

Sagrada Familia

wild boar

•Barcelona

SPAIN

Ebro R.

grapes

bullfighting

olives

oil rig

■ MADRID

oranges

BALEARIC ISLANDS (SPAIN)

MINORCA

•Mahón

•Toledo

MAJORCA

•Palma

windmill

•Valencia

sunflowers

almonds

IBIZA

flamenco dancers

fishing boat

Alhambra Palace

•Almeria

sardines

Most Spanish people live in towns and cities, but many make their living from farming or fishing. Tourism is a major industry in Spain and Portugal, and both countries attract vacationers year round. Most of the world's supply of cork is produced by these two countries.

tuna

MEDITERRANEAN SEA

France

France is one of Europe's largest farming and industrial countries. Its mild climate becomes hotter and drier toward its mountainous borders with Italy and Spain. France is famous for its fine food and wines.

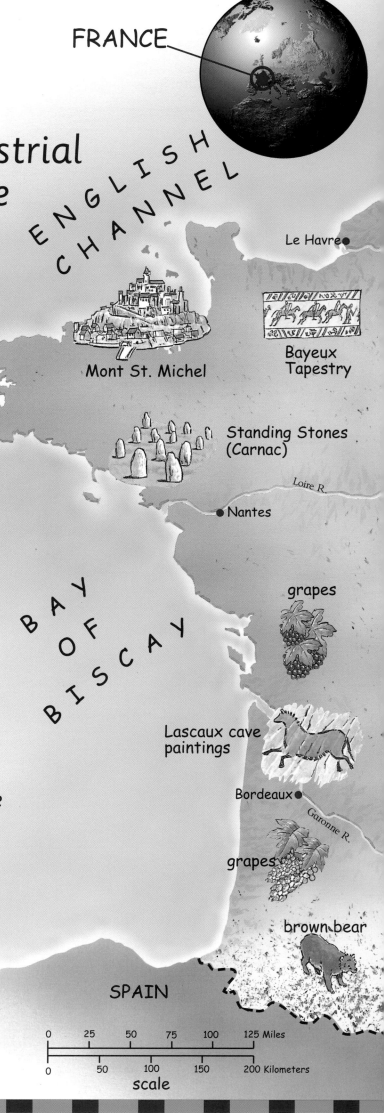

FRANCE

ENGLISH CHANNEL

Le Havre

Mont St. Michel

Bayeux Tapestry

Standing Stones (Carnac)

Loire R.

Nantes

BAY OF BISCAY

grapes

Lascaux cave paintings

Bordeaux

Garonne R.

grapes

brown bear

SPAIN

0	25	50	75	100	125 Miles
0	50	100	150	200 Kilometers

scale

Can you find...

the Eiffel Tower?

the amphitheater at Arles?

Mont St. Michel?

Much of France is farmland, but most people now live in towns and cities.

The area around Paris, the capital city, is densely populated. Paris is famous for its great fashion houses and fine restaurants, and as a center for the arts.

Andorra and Monaco are small, independent countries. Many wealthy people choose to live in Monaco because of its tax laws.

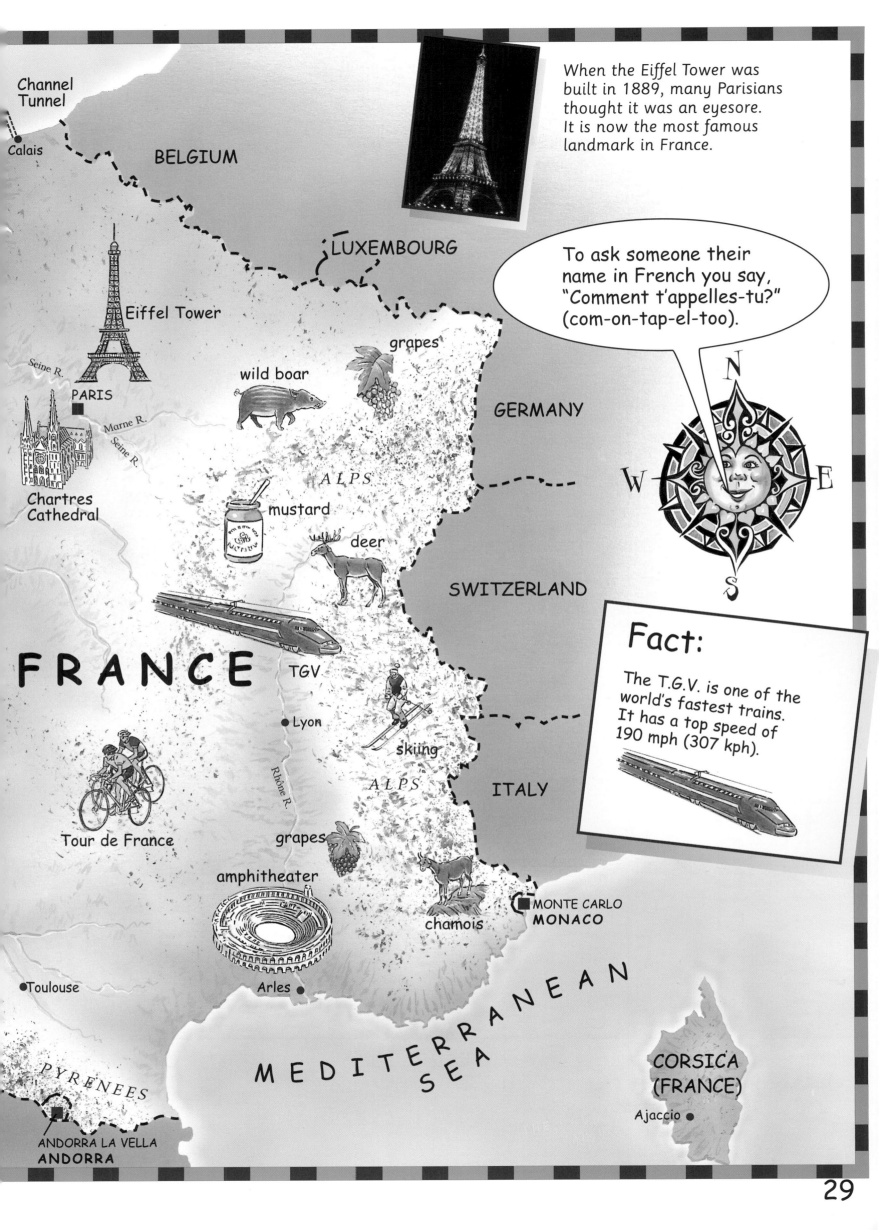

Channel Tunnel

Calais

BELGIUM

LUXEMBOURG

Eiffel Tower

Seine R.

PARIS

Marne R.

Seine R.

Chartres Cathedral

grapes

wild boar

GERMANY

ALPS

mustard

deer

SWITZERLAND

FRANCE

TGV

Lyon

skiing

ALPS

ITALY

Rhône R.

Tour de France

grapes

amphitheater

chamois

MONTE CARLO
MONACO

Toulouse

Arles

MEDITERRANEAN SEA

PYRENEES

ANDORRA LA VELLA
ANDORRA

CORSICA (FRANCE)

Ajaccio

When the Eiffel Tower was built in 1889, many Parisians thought it was an eyesore. It is now the most famous landmark in France.

To ask someone their name in French you say, "Comment t'appelles-tu?" (com-on-tap-el-too).

N

W E

S

Fact:

The T.G.V. is one of the world's fastest trains. It has a top speed of 190 mph (307 kph).

Belgium, Netherlands, and Luxembourg

This part of Europe is called the Low Countries. Most of the land in these countries is flat. Large areas of land have been reclaimed from the sea by draining it and building long dykes (walls) to protect the land from flooding.

Belgium is famous for lacemaking and fine chocolate.

N E
W S

BELGIUM, NETHERLANDS, AND LUXEMBOURG

windmill

clogs

ice skating

seal

NETHERLANDS

GERMANY

Ijssel R.

canal house

AMSTERDAM

Delft pottery

Edam cheese

diamond cutting

tulips

Rotterdam

Lek R.

The Hague

NORTH SEA

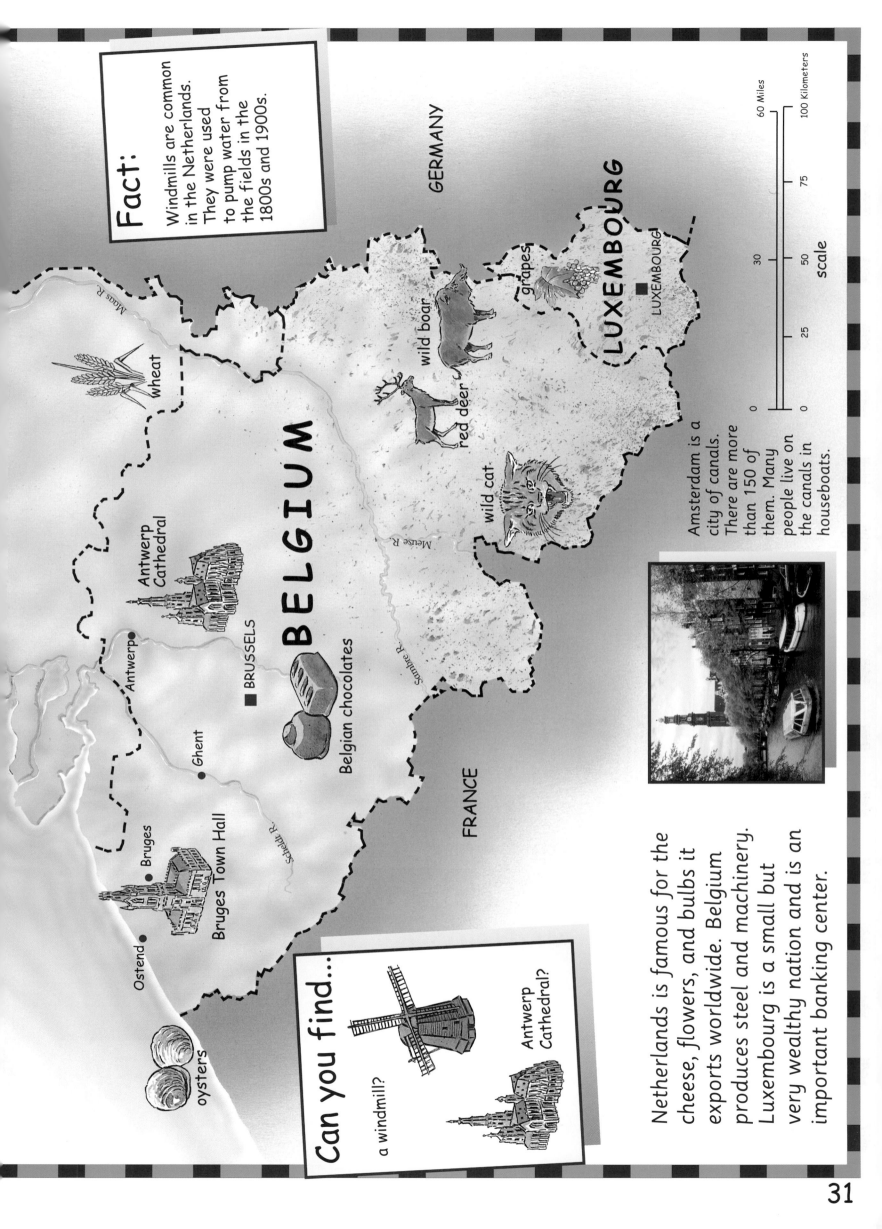

Fact:

Windmills are common in the Netherlands. They were used to pump water from the fields in the 1800s and 1900s.

GERMANY

LUXEMBOURG

LUXEMBOURG

Maas R.

wheat

wild boar

red deer

grapes

wild cat

Meuse R.

Antwerp Cathedral

BELGIUM

■ BRUSSELS

Belgian chocolates

Antwerp●

Sambre R.

Ghent●

●Bruges

Bruges Town Hall

Schelde R.

Ostend●

oysters

FRANCE

60 Miles

100 Kilometers

0   25   30   50   75

0

scale

Amsterdam is a city of canals. There are more than 150 of them. Many people live on the canals in houseboats.

Can you find...

a windmill?

Antwerp Cathedral?

Netherlands is famous for the cheese, flowers, and bulbs it exports worldwide. Belgium produces steel and machinery. Luxembourg is a small but very wealthy nation and is an important banking center.

31

Neuschwanstein Castle was built by King Louis II. Walt Disney based his fairy-tale castle on this fantastic building.

GERMANY, AUSTRIA, AND SWITZERLAND

NORTH SEA

NETHERLANDS

Weser R.

sausages

Rhine R.

Cologne Cathedral

● Düsseldorf

● Cologne

● Bonn

Beethoven's birthplace

BELGIUM

LUXEMBOURG

Roman ruins

FRANCE

cuckoo clock

grapes

Zurich ●

watch

Gruyère cheese

■ BERNE

SWITZERLAND

L. Geneva

chocolates

Germany, Austria, and Switzerland

Germany is a wealthy industrial nation. It produces cars and electrical goods. It has a large population and many large cities. There are forests, long rivers, and lots of castles. Germany's large rivers are important for transporting goods around the country.

| 0 | 25 | 50 | 75 | 100 | 125 Miles |

| 0 | 50 | 100 | 150 | 200 Kilometers |

scale

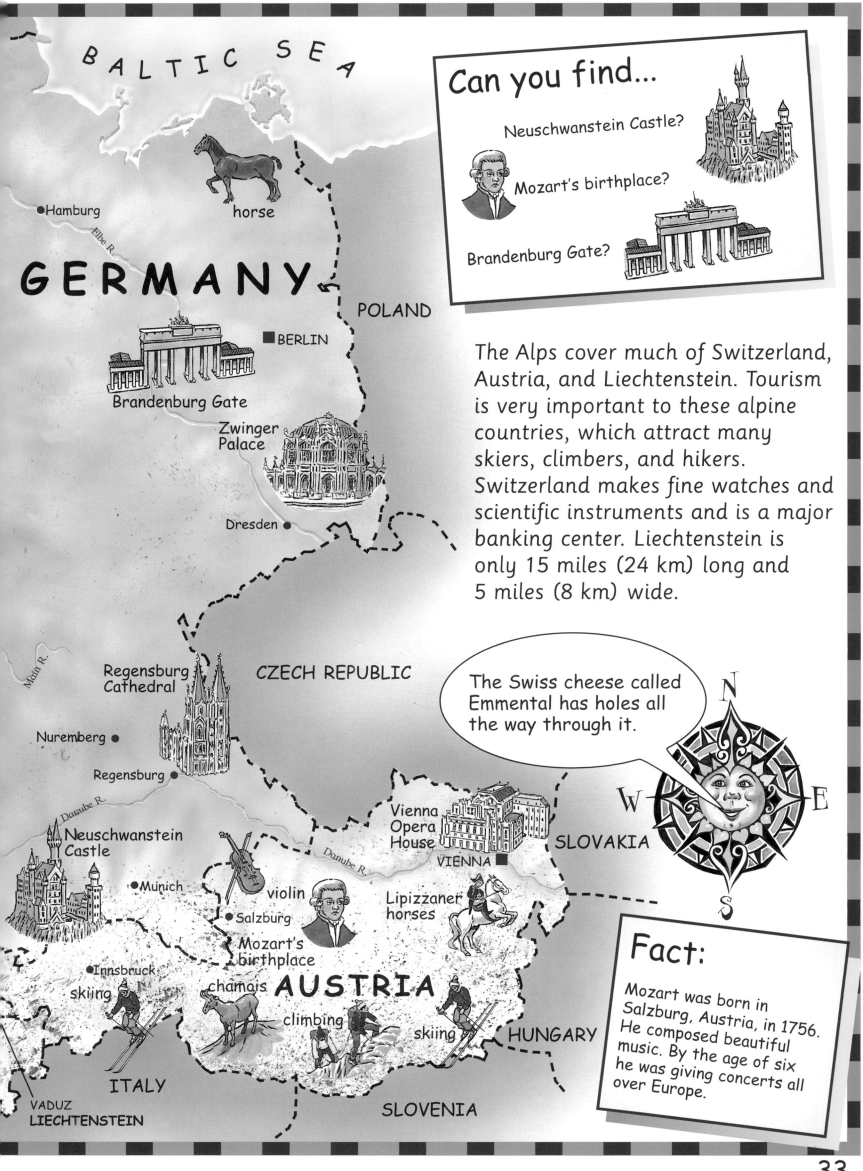

BALTIC SEA

horse

•Hamburg

Elbe R.

GERMANY

POLAND

■BERLIN

Brandenburg Gate

Zwinger Palace

Dresden •

Main R.

Regensburg Cathedral

CZECH REPUBLIC

Nuremberg •

Regensburg •

Danube R.

Neuschwanstein Castle

violin

• Munich

Salzburg

Mozart's birthplace

• Innsbruck

skiing

chamois AUSTRIA

climbing

ITALY

VADUZ
LIECHTENSTEIN

Vienna Opera House

Danube R.

VIENNA ■

Lipizzaner horses

SLOVAKIA

skiing

HUNGARY

SLOVENIA

Can you find...

Neuschwanstein Castle?

Mozart's birthplace?

Brandenburg Gate?

The Alps cover much of Switzerland, Austria, and Liechtenstein. Tourism is very important to these alpine countries, which attract many skiers, climbers, and hikers. Switzerland makes fine watches and scientific instruments and is a major banking center. Liechtenstein is only 15 miles (24 km) long and 5 miles (8 km) wide.

The Swiss cheese called Emmental has holes all the way through it.

N
W   E
S

Fact:

Mozart was born in Salzburg, Austria, in 1756. He composed beautiful music. By the age of six he was giving concerts all over Europe.

33

Italy and Malta

Italy is famous for its art, food, fashion, and cars. Most of its population, industry, and farmland are concentrated along the Po River in the north.

Fact:

Pizza is a traditional food that was invented in Italy. It is now eaten worldwide.

Can you find...

Pompeii?   the Leaning Tower of Pisa?   the Colosseum?

125 Miles
200 Kilometers
scale
0 25 50 75 100 125
0 50 100 150 200

SWITZERLAND

AUSTRIA

SLOVENIA

CROATIA

ALPS

ALPS

FRANCE

Milan Cathedral
• Milan

violin

L. Garda

St. Mark's Square

Venice

gondolier

Po R.

pasta

Parma ham

Parmesan cheese

Turin

grapes

olives

Leaning Tower of Pisa
• Pisa

Florence Cathedral
• Florence

Tiber R.

SAN MARINO
SAN MARINO

ITALY

Colosseum

Vatican City

ROME
VATICAN CITY

CORSICA (FRANCE)

LIGURIAN SEA

ADRIATIC SEA

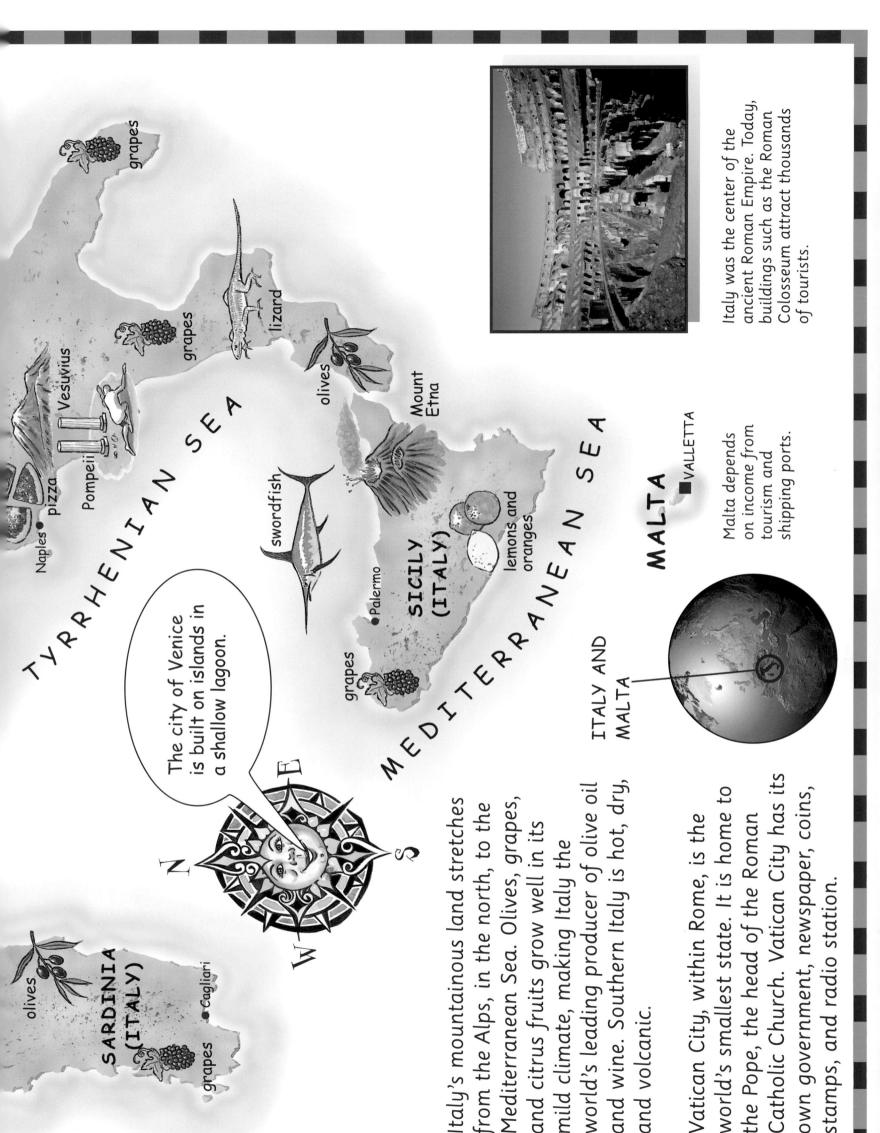

grapes

Vesuvius

grapes

lizard

pizza

Pompeii

Naples •

olives

Mount Etna

TYRRHENIAN SEA

swordfish

SICILY (ITALY)

Palermo •

lemons and oranges

MEDITERRANEAN SEA

grapes

The city of Venice is built on islands in a shallow lagoon.

N E W S

SARDINIA (ITALY)

olives

Cagliari •

grapes

Italy was the center of the ancient Roman Empire. Today, buildings such as the Roman Colosseum attract thousands of tourists.

MALTA

■ VALLETTA

Malta depends on income from tourism and shipping ports.

ITALY AND MALTA

Italy's mountainous land stretches from the Alps, in the north, to the Mediterranean Sea. Olives, grapes, and citrus fruits grow well in its mild climate, making Italy the world's leading producer of olive oil and wine. Southern Italy is hot, dry, and volcanic.

Vatican City, within Rome, is the world's smallest state. It is home to the Pope, the head of the Roman Catholic Church. Vatican City has its own government, newspaper, coins, stamps, and radio station.

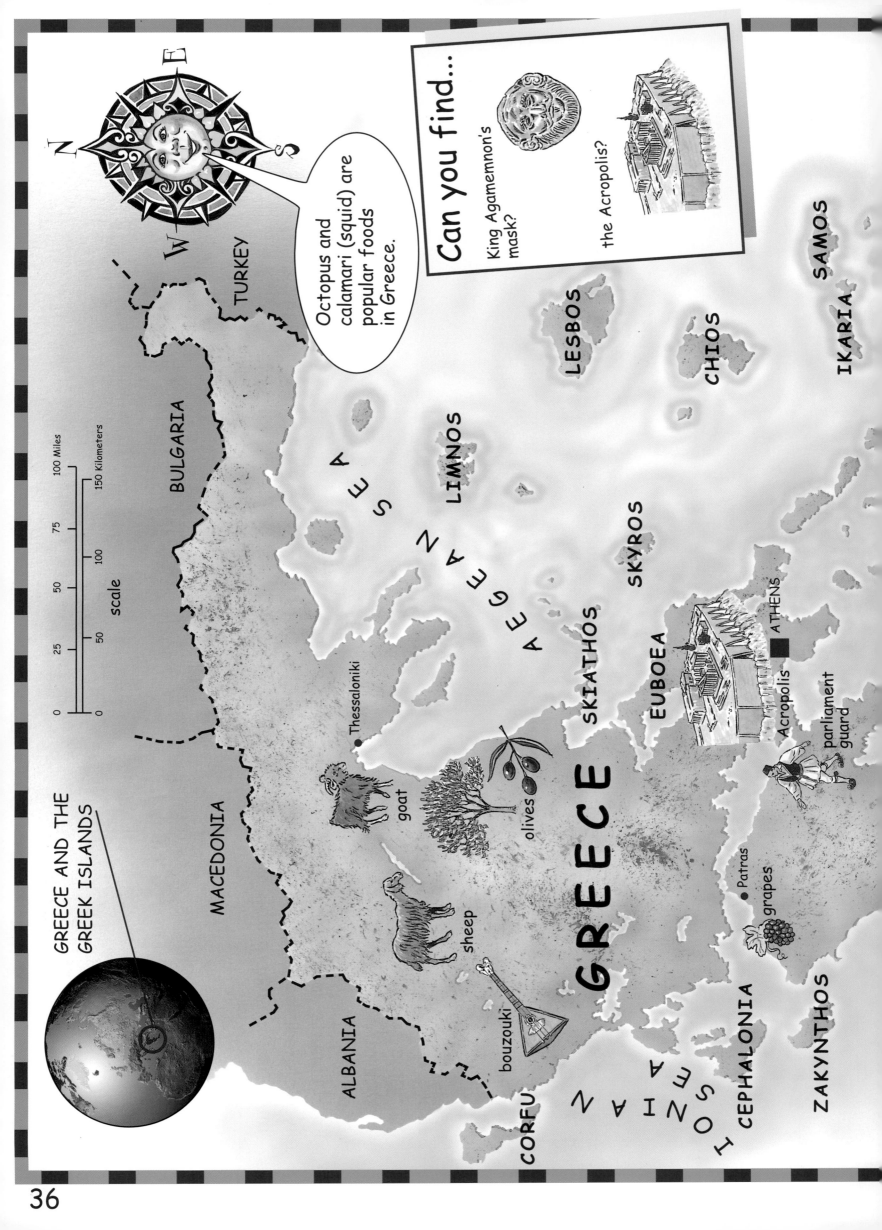

GREECE AND THE GREEK ISLANDS

Octopus and calamari (squid) are popular foods in Greece.

Can you find...

King Agamemnon's mask?

the Acropolis?

TURKEY

BULGARIA

MACEDONIA

ALBANIA

AEGEAN SEA

LESBOS

CHIOS

SAMOS

IKARIA

LIMNOS

SKYROS

SKIATHOS

EUBOEA

ATHENS

Acropolis

parliament guard

GREECE

Thessaloniki

goat

olives

sheep

Patras

grapes

bouzouki

CORFU

CEPHALONIA

ZAKYNTHOS

IONIAN SEA

scale

100 Miles

150 Kilometers

75

100

50

50

25

50

0

0

N E S W

36

Greece and the Greek Islands

Greece is in southern Europe. It is a dry, mountainous country with many islands. The capital city, Athens, is home to more than one-third of Greece's population. Farming and tourism are the major industries.

King Agamemnon's mask

olives

octopus

NAXOS

THIRA

dolphins

Irá Klion

olives

CRETE

grapes

KOS

RHODES

AEGEAN SEA

MEDITERRANEAN

The Ancient Greeks were Europe's first great civilization. Each year, thousands of tourists explore Greece's ancient buildings and archaeological sites. Greece is a popular vacation destination, attracting many visitors with its scenery, sunshine, and fine beaches. Its hot climate is ideal for growing olives, grapes, and citrus fruits.

The Parthenon is an ancient Greek temple. It stands on the Acropolis, a rocky hill that towers over the city of Athens.

The south of the region is rugged and mountainous with many areas of rich farmland. In 1993 Czechoslovakia split into two countries: the Czech Republic and Slovakia. Slovenia, Bosnia and Herzegovina, Croatia, and Macedonia were all once part of Yugoslavia. They have recently become independent countries.

Hungarian goulash is a dish made of beef, paprika, and sour cream.

150 Miles
200 Kilometers
100
100
scale
50
0
0

N
E
W
S

Can you find...

Alexander Nevsky Cathedral?

Bratislava Castle?

BALTIC SEA

RUSSIA
LITHUANIA
BELARUS

Windmill

POLAND

European bison

■ WARSAW

Cracow

skiing

brown bear

UKRAINE

PRAGUE

CZECH REPUBLIC

Bratislava Castle

SLOVAKIA

■ BRATISLAVA

Danube R.

Budapest Parliament

■ BUDAPEST

HUNGARY

wild cat

GERMANY

AUSTRIA

SLOVENIA

CENTRAL AND EASTERN EUROPE

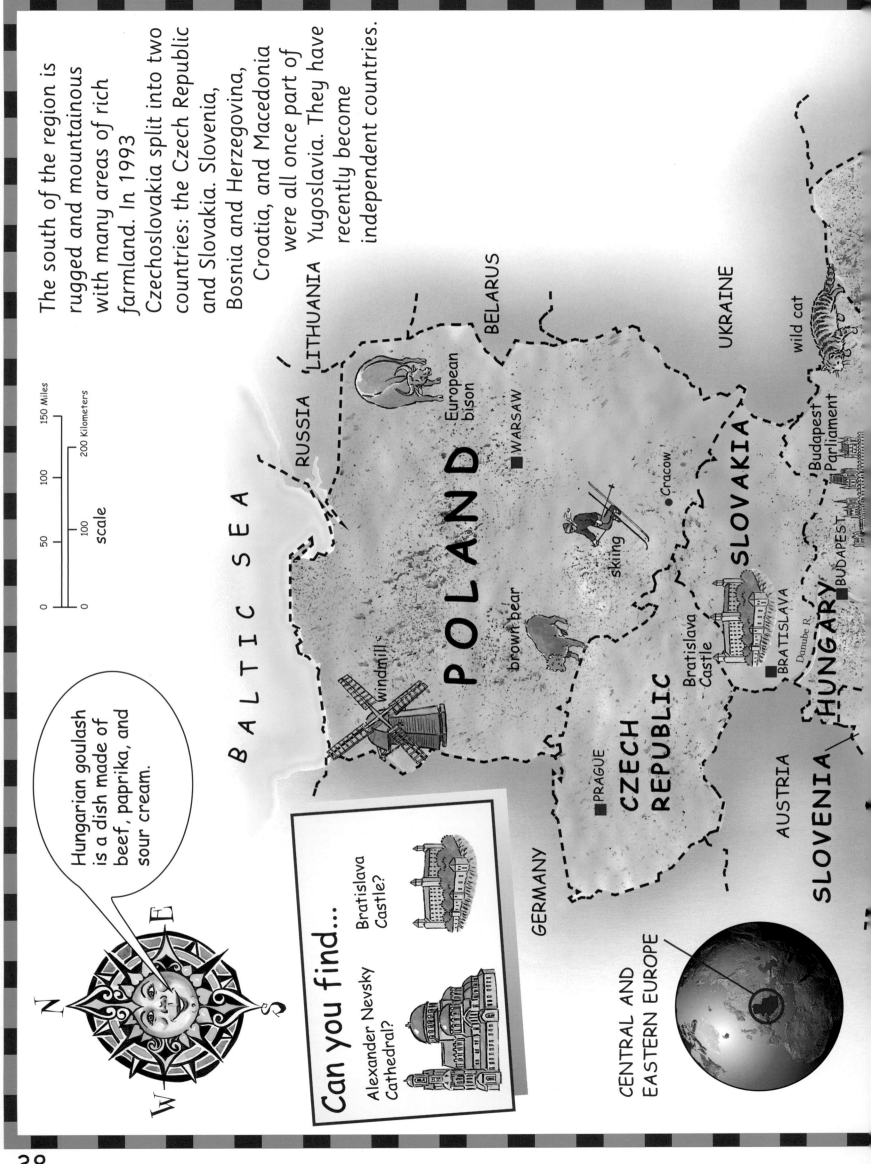

Central and Eastern Europe

Parts of this region suffered bitter fighting during the 1990s. Borders were redrawn, and new countries have been created. Poland is the largest and most populated country in the region. It has major iron, steel, and shipbuilding industries.

MOLDOVA

TRANSYLVANIA

BLACK SEA

Bran Castle

R. Danube

BUCHAREST

Alexander Nevsky Cathedral

TURKEY

sunflowers

ROMANIA

SOFIA

BULGARIA

SERBIA

SKOPJE

BELGRADE

MACEDONIA

Sava R.

PRISTINA

BOSNIA AND HERZEGOVINA

YUGOSLAVIA

KOSOVO

GREECE

SARAJEVO

Skiing

CROATIA

ZAGREB

MONTENEGRO

PODGORICA

TIRANA

ALBANIA

Dubrovnik

Split

Roman amphitheater

ADRIATIC SEA

ITALY

Northern Eurasia

This vast region stretches across Asia and Europe. Until 1991 it was one single country, the Soviet Union. Today, it is made up of fifteen independent nations including Russia, the largest country in the world.

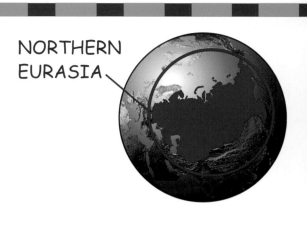

NORTHERN EURASIA

B A R E N T S S E A

ice-breaker

polar bear

FINLAND

Winter Palace

TALLIN

ESTONIA

Kremlin

LATVIA

RIGA

LITHUANIA

VILNIUS

R U S S I A

POLAND

MINSK

BELARUS

MOSCOW

St. Basil's Cathedral

U R A L   M O U N T A I N S

woolly mammoth fossils

oil

SLOVAKIA
HUNGARY
MOLDOVA
ROMANIA
BULGARIA

KIEV

UKRAINE

Don R.

Fabergé egg

balalaika

Yenisey R.

ballet

B L A C K   S E A

caviar

ox

nomad yurt

TURKEY

C A S P I A N   S E A

KAZAKHSTAN

ASTANA

TBILISI

GEORGIA

camel

snow leopard

YEREVAN

BAKU

ARMENIA

AZERBAIJAN

TASHKENT

CHINA

Turk horseman

UZBEKISTAN

BISHKEK

ASHGABAT

cotton

IRAN

KYRGYZSTAN

DUSHANBE

TURKMENISTAN

AFGHANISTAN

TAJIKISTAN

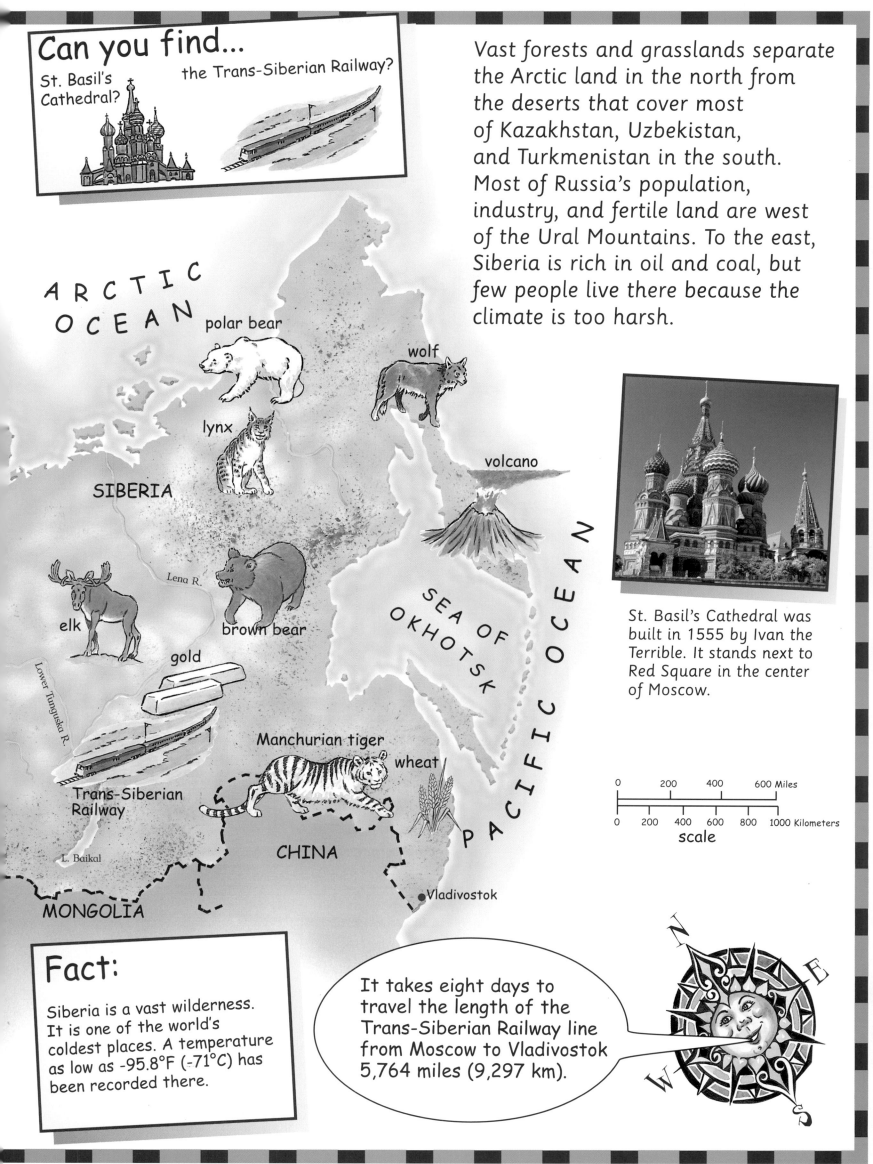

Can you find...

St. Basil's Cathedral?

the Trans-Siberian Railway?

Vast forests and grasslands separate the Arctic land in the north from the deserts that cover most of Kazakhstan, Uzbekistan, and Turkmenistan in the south. Most of Russia's population, industry, and fertile land are west of the Ural Mountains. To the east, Siberia is rich in oil and coal, but few people live there because the climate is too harsh.

ARCTIC OCEAN

polar bear

wolf

lynx

volcano

SIBERIA

Lena R.

elk

brown bear

gold

Lower Tunguska R.

SEA OF OKHOTSK

PACIFIC OCEAN

St. Basil's Cathedral was built in 1555 by Ivan the Terrible. It stands next to Red Square in the center of Moscow.

Manchurian tiger

wheat

Trans-Siberian Railway

L. Baikal

CHINA

Vladivostok

MONGOLIA

scale

0   200   400   600 Miles
0   200   400   600   800   1000 Kilometers

Fact:

Siberia is a vast wilderness. It is one of the world's coldest places. A temperature as low as -95.8°F (-71°C) has been recorded there.

It takes eight days to travel the length of the Trans-Siberian Railway line from Moscow to Vladivostok 5,764 miles (9,297 km).

Can you find...

the Royal Tomb at Petra?

the Suleymaniye Mosque?

SOUTHWEST ASIA

Southwest Asia

This area, also known as the Middle East, is mainly hot and dry with vast arid deserts in the south. This region supplies much of the world's oil.

The Middle East has long been troubled by wars between neighboring countries. Large amounts of oil and natural gas around the Persian Gulf has brought great wealth to the region.

Fact:

The Dead Sea lies on the border of Israel and Jordan. Its water is so salty that people can float in it without swimming. It is impossible to sink!

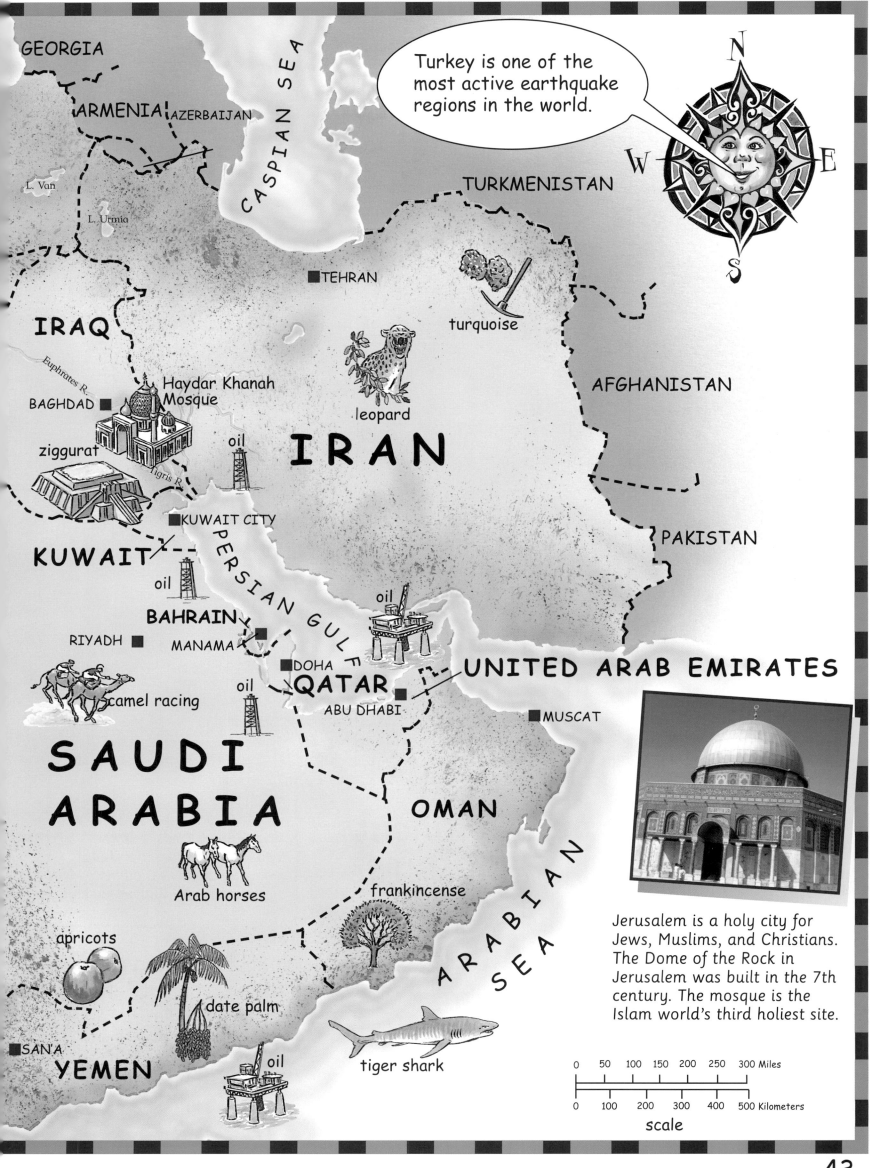

GEORGIA

ARMENIA AZERBAIJAN

CASPIAN SEA

L. Van

L. Urmia

TURKMENISTAN

Turkey is one of the most active earthquake regions in the world.

N
W E
S

TEHRAN

turquoise

IRAQ

AFGHANISTAN

Euphrates R.

BAGHDAD

Haydar Khanah Mosque

leopard

IRAN

ziggurat

Tigris R.

oil

PAKISTAN

KUWAIT CITY

KUWAIT

oil

P E R S I A N   G U L F

BAHRAIN

RIYADH

MANAMA

oil

oil

DOHA

QATAR

ABU DHABI

UNITED ARAB EMIRATES

MUSCAT

camel racing

S A U D I
A R A B I A

OMAN

Arab horses

frankincense

A R A B I A N

S E A

Jerusalem is a holy city for Jews, Muslims, and Christians. The Dome of the Rock in Jerusalem was built in the 7th century. The mosque is the Islam world's third holiest site.

apricots

date palm

tiger shark

SAN'A

YEMEN

oil

| 0 | 50 | 100 | 150 | 200 | 250 | 300 Miles |

| 0 | 100 | 200 | 300 | 400 | 500 Kilometers |

scale

43

NORTHERN AFRICA

Tangier

ALGIERS

TUNIS

RABAT

TUNISIA

CANARY
ISLANDS
(SPAIN)

MOROCCO

TRIPOLI

ALGERIA

WESTERN
SAHARA

nomads

LIBYA

(disputed)

oil

S A H A R A

dolphins

MAURITANIA

ostrich

NOUAKCHOTT

MALI

SENEGAL

hippopotamus

Niger R.

GAMBIA

DAKAR

NIGER

BANJUL

BAMAKO

NIAMEY

L. Chad

**GUINEA-
BISSAU**

**BURKINA
FASO**

BISSAU

GUINEA

OUAGADOUGOU

N'DJAMENA

CONAKRY

diamonds

NIGERIA

Niger R.

FREETOWN

ABUJA

**SIERRA
LEONE**

bananas

GHANA

MONROVIA

LIBERIA

ACCRA

YAOUNDÉ

LOMÉ

PORTO-
NOVO

oil

YAMOUSSOUKRO

CÔTE D'IVOIRE

TOGO

CAMEROON

BENIN

GABON

A T L A N T I C   O C E A N

Northern Africa

Much of the huge continent of Africa is hot and dry. The land along the Mediterranean Sea and the Nile Valley is rich and fertile. The vast Sahara Desert covers more than half of north Africa.

Fact:

The Sahara Desert is the largest desert in the world, covering about 5.6 million square miles (9 million sq. km).

Many Africans live in small villages and farm the land. The Nile Valley in Egypt is the most densely populated region. Cairo is Africa's largest city.

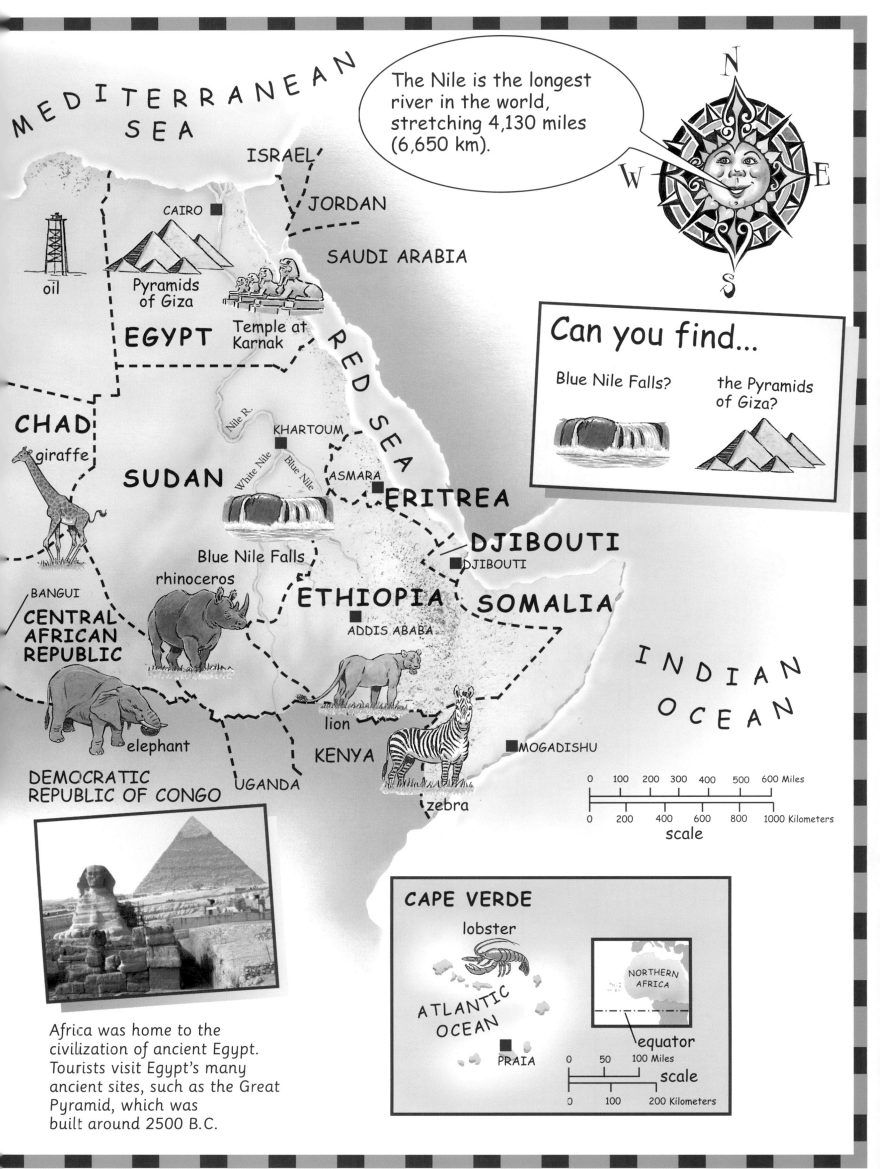

MEDITERRANEAN SEA

The Nile is the longest river in the world, stretching 4,130 miles (6,650 km).

N
W E
S

ISRAEL

JORDAN

SAUDI ARABIA

oil

CAIRO ■

Pyramids of Giza

Temple at Karnak

EGYPT

RED SEA

Nile R.

KHARTOUM ■

White Nile   Blue Nile

ASMARA ■

CHAD

giraffe

SUDAN

ERITREA

DJIBOUTI

DJIBOUTI ■

Blue Nile Falls

rhinoceros

ETHIOPIA

SOMALIA

BANGUI

CENTRAL AFRICAN REPUBLIC

ADDIS ABABA ■

INDIAN OCEAN

elephant

lion

DEMOCRATIC REPUBLIC OF CONGO

UGANDA

KENYA

zebra

■ MOGADISHU

Can you find...

Blue Nile Falls?   the Pyramids of Giza?

| 0 | 100 | 200 | 300 | 400 | 500 | 600 Miles |

| 0 | 200 | 400 | 600 | 800 | 1000 Kilometers |

scale

Africa was home to the civilization of ancient Egypt. Tourists visit Egypt's many ancient sites, such as the Great Pyramid, which was built around 2500 B.C.

CAPE VERDE

lobster

ATLANTIC OCEAN

NORTHERN AFRICA

equator

PRAIA ■

| 0 | 50 | 100 Miles |

scale

| 0 | 100 | 200 Kilometers |

The top of Mount Kilimanjaro in Tanzania is covered in snow year-round.

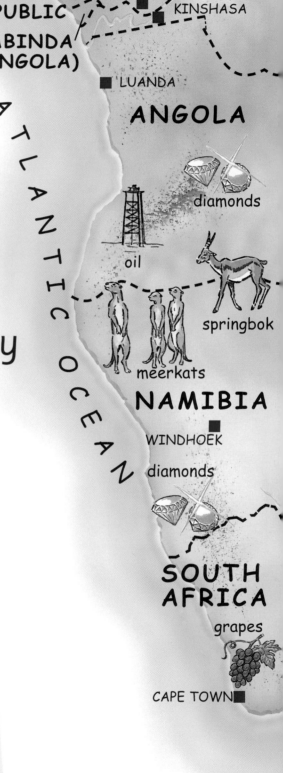

EQUATORIAL GUINEA
MALABO
CAMEROON
pygmies
chimpanzee
LIBREVILLE
GABON
flying fish
CONGO REPUBLIC
BRAZZAVILLE
rain forest
KINSHASA
CABINDA (ANGOLA)
LUANDA
ANGOLA
ATLANTIC OCEAN
diamonds
oil
springbok
meerkats
NAMIBIA
WINDHOEK
diamonds
SOUTH AFRICA
grapes
CAPE TOWN

Southern Africa

The mighty Congo River runs through dense, tropical rain forests in Central Africa. Crocodiles, chimpanzees, and gorillas live in these hot, steamy forests. Grasslands and deserts make up much of Southern Africa, but there is also rich farmland in the far south.

Can you find...

Victoria Falls?

meerkats?

Fact:

Pygmy tribes live deep in the rain forests of Congo. They are a race of people who are mostly under 5 feet (1.5 m) tall.

```
0    100   200   300   400   500   600 Miles
|----|----|----|----|----|----|----|

0        200      400      600      800    1000 Kilometers
|--------|--------|--------|--------|--------|
                    scale
```

SUDAN

ETHIOPIA

DEMOCRATIC REPUBLIC OF CONGO

Ankole cattle

SOMALIA

KENYA

UGANDA

Congo (Zaire) R.

KAMPALA

NAIROBI

KIGALI

L. Victoria

RWANDA

Mt. Kilimanjaro

BUJUMBURA

BURUNDI

cheetah

great white shark

TANZANIA

L. Tanganyika

Zanzibar

bananas

DAR ES SALAAM

giraffe

cashew nuts

SEYCHELLES

VICTORIA

elephant

COMOROS

ZAMBIA

MALAWI

LILONGWE

MORONI

LUSAKA

Victoria Falls

L. Nyasa

coconuts

HARARE

Zambezi R.

aardvark

MOZAMBIQUE

ANTANANARIVO

ZIMBABWE

MADAGASCAR

MAURITIUS

BOTSWANA

Orange R.

Cape buffalo

SAINT-DENIS

rugby

GABORONE

RÉUNION

PORT LOUIS

PRETORIA

MAPUTO

MBABANE

chameleon

SWAZILAND

gold

MASERU

LESOTHO

BLOEMFONTEIN

INDIAN OCEAN

SOUTHERN AFRICA

Africa is the world's second-largest continent and is made up of many countries. South Africa is rich in copper, gold, and diamonds, making it the continent's wealthiest country. It is also an important farming region. Large nature reserves have been created all over southern Africa to protect some of its wild animals. The land is home to zebras, lions, cheetahs, leopards, elephants, rhinoceroses, ostriches, and giraffes.

TURKMENISTAN TAJIKISTAN

Kashmir goat

carpet

disputed border

AFGHANISTAN

KABUL ■

ISLAMABAD ■

yak

CHINA

woman wearing burkha

Khyber Pass

Badshahi Mosque

Golden Temple

HIMALAYAS

PAKISTAN

IRAN

tomb of Mohammed Ali Jinnah

Indus R.

Parliament House

NEPAL

camels

NEW DELHI ■

KATHMANDU

Karachi ●

Jaipur ●

Agra ●

Ganges R.

rhinoceros

Varanasi ●

Palace of the Winds

Narmada R.

sitar

Ahmadabad ●

INDIA

cotton

Hindu dancer

A
R
A
B
I
A
N

S
E
A

Mumbai (Bombay) ●

peacock

Godavari R.

sari

Krishna R.

temple elephant

rice

Bangalore ●

India and Its Neighbors

More than 950 million people live in India. It is the largest country in the region. Most people work on the land, but exports of cars and electronic goods are growing in importance.

tea

sloth

COLOMBO ■

SRI LANKA

Can you find...

the Pclace of the Winds?

the Golden Temple?

a temple elephant?

Vast mountain ranges separate this region from central Asia. The climate is hot and dry, so many people live on the coast or on the fertile plains along the Ganges and Indus Rivers. India, Bangladesh, and Sri Lanka are some of the world's main tea-growing nations. Most industries are concentrated in India and Pakistan's large, crowded cities.

BHUTAN

Mt. Everest

THIMPHU

Brahmaputra R.

tea

INDIA

BANGLADESH

Ganges R. DHAKA

Kolkatta (Calcutta)

BAY OF BENGAL

CHINA

logging elephant

MYANMAR (BURMA)

LAOS

Irrawaddy R.

THAILAND

Buddhist monk

YANGON (RANGOON)

INDIAN OCEAN

rubber trees

Mount Everest, in the Himalayas, is the tallest mountain in the world. It is 29,028 feet (8,848 m) tall.

ANDAMAN AND NICOBAR ISLANDS

Fact:

Indian cobras are poisonous snakes. They can grow up to 18 feet (5.5 m) long.

| 0 | 100 | 200 | 300 | 400 | 500 | 600 Miles |

scale

| 0 | 200 | 400 | 600 | 800 | 1000 Kilometers |

Japan

Japan is made up of four large islands and thousands of smaller ones. It lies off the east coast of China. Japan's cities are built along its flat coastland because mountains and forests cover much of the country inland.

Twenty-seven million people live in Tokyo, Japan's capital city.

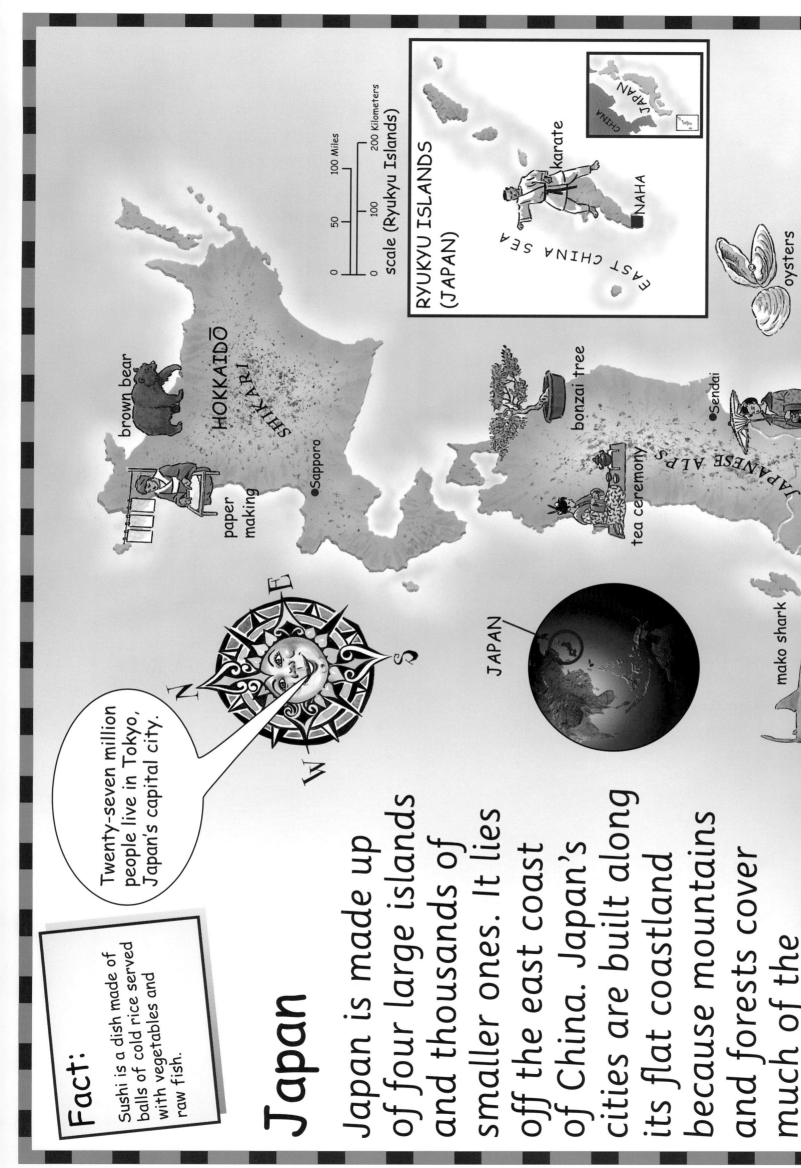

RYUKYU ISLANDS (JAPAN)

scale (Ryukyu Islands)

200 Kilometers
100 Miles

100
50

0
0

EAST CHINA SEA

NAHA

karate

CHINA

JAPAN

HOKKAIDŌ

SHIKARI

brown bear

paper making

•Sapporo

bonzai tree

tea ceremony

JAPANESE ALPS

HONSHŪ

•Sendai

women's traditional costume

oysters

mako shark

JAPAN

N
E
S
W

Can you find...

Mt. Fuji?

Osaka Castle?

Torii Gate?

Japan is a major industrial nation. It makes more cars and cameras than any other country and exports many electrical goods. It is one of the richest countries in Asia. Northern Japan is cold, but the southern climate is tropical. Earthquakes are common in Japan, and the country is often hit by fierce storms called typhoons.

TOKYO

Yokohama

JAPAN

Mt. Fuji

pearls

O C E A N

Temple of the Golden Pavilion

L. Biwa

Kyoto

Osaka

Kobe

chopsticks

Osaka Castle

swordfish

P A C I F I C

Hiroshima

SHIKOKU

octopus

Torii Gate

kendo

KYŪSHŪ

Kagoshima

S E A   O F
J A P A N
(E A S T   S E A)

scale

0   25   50   75   100 Miles

0   50   100   150 Kilometers

Mount Fuji is the highest volcano in Japan, reaching 12,388 feet (3,776 m) at its summit. According to legend, an earthquake created Mt. Fuji in 286 B.C. Its last big eruption was in 1707.

Oil-rich Brunei is one of the world's smallest and wealthiest countries.

Southeast Asia

Southeast Asia is made up of two small areas of mainland and almost twenty thousand islands. The climate is hot and humid. Tropical rain forests cover much of this mountainous region and provide the world with most of its hardwoods.

CHINA

elephant

VIETNAM

HANOI

MYANMAR (BURMA)

LAOS

VIENTIANE

folk dancer

THAILAND

BANGKOK

Angkor Wat

CAMBODIA

PHNOM PENH

Ho Chi Minh City

ANDAMAN SEA

rubber tree

leather back turtle

MALAYSIA

KUALA LUMPUR

tiger

SINGAPORE

SUMATRA

tea

INDIAN OCEAN

JAKARTA

JAVA

Can you find...

Angkor Wat?

the skyscrapers of Singapore?

SOUTHEAST ASIA

In remote areas of Southeast Asia, people live in houses raised on stilts to avoid being flooded during the rainy season. Monsoon rains fall from June to October. The climate is ideal for growing rice, Southeast Asia's main crop. Pineapples, bananas, mangos, and coconuts are also grown.
The rain forests are rich in plantlife and are home to orangutans, rhinoceroses, leopards, and tigers.

tiger shark

swordfish

■ MANILA

PHILIPPINES

pineapple

MINDANAO

BRUNEI
BANDAR SERI
BEGAWAN
■ MALAYSIA

head hunter
with blowpipe

BORNEO

rice

CELEBES

coconuts

coffee

oil rig

house on stilts

IRIAN JAYA

PAPUA NEW
GUINEA

PACIFIC OCEAN

0   100   200   300   400   500   600 Miles

0   200   400   600   800   1000 Kilometers
scale

I N D O N E S I A

Borobudur
Temple

shadow puppet

Komodo dragon

TIMOR

hammerhead shark

AUSTRALIA

China, Mongolia, Korea, and Taiwan

CHINA, MONGOLIA, KOREA, AND TAIWAN

More people live in China than in any other country on Earth. Most of the population farms the fertile land in the east, growing rice, wheat, corn, and tea. China is also an industrial nation with many large cities.

High mountain ranges separate China from India, and there are vast deserts to the north. The Korean peninsula is divided into North and South Korea. South Korea and the island of Taiwan have successful industries, including textiles, cars, and electronics.

KAZAKHSTAN

oil

wheat

KYRGYZSTAN

cotton

TAJIKISTAN

jade

PAKISTAN

giant panda

INDIA

XIZANG (TIBET)

Tibetan monk

HIMALAYAS

NEPAL

BHUTA

INDIA

The Great Wall of China is 2,145 miles (3,460 km) long. It is the only man-made structure that can be seen from the Moon.

Can you find...

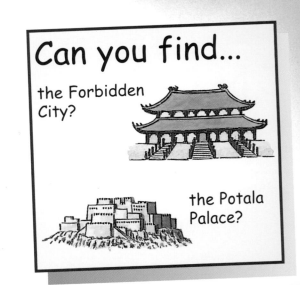

the Forbidden City?

the Potala Palace?

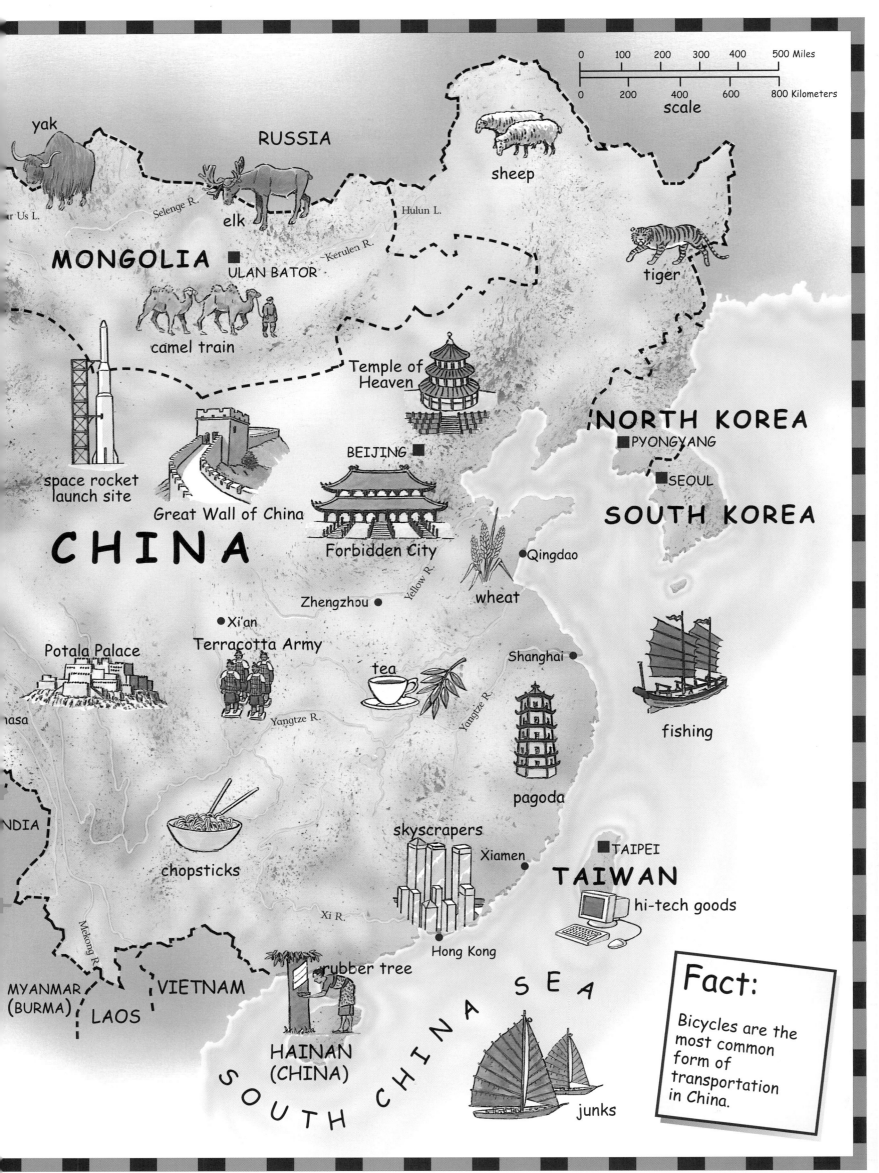

yak

RUSSIA

sheep

Selenge R.

elk

ar Us L.

Hulun L.

Kerulen R.

tiger

MONGOLIA   ■ ULAN BATOR

camel train

space rocket launch site

Temple of Heaven

Great Wall of China

BEIJING   ■

NORTH KOREA

■ PYONGYANG

■ SEOUL

CHINA

Forbidden City

SOUTH KOREA

Yellow R.

•Qingdao

Zhengzhou •

wheat

Potala Palace

•Xi'an

Terracotta Army

tea

Shanghai •

hasa

Yangtze R.

Yangtze R.

fishing

pagoda

chopsticks

skyscrapers

Xiamen •

■ TAIPEI

TAIWAN

Xi R.

hi-tech goods

NDIA

Mekong R.

rubber tree

Hong Kong

MYANMAR (BURMA)

VIETNAM

LAOS

HAINAN (CHINA)

SOUTH CHINA SEA

junks

scale

Fact:

Bicycles are the most common form of transportation in China.

AUSTRALIA AND
PAPUA NEW GUINEA

Papua New Guinea has over seven hundred languages — more than any other country.

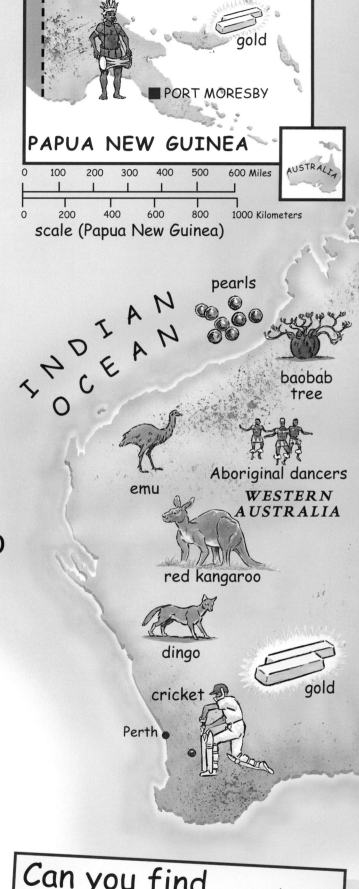

traditional dancer

gold

■ PORT MORESBY

PAPUA NEW GUINEA

AUSTRALIA

```
0    100   200   300   400   500   600 Miles
```
```
0    200    400    600    800    1000 Kilometers
```
scale (Papua New Guinea)

pearls

INDIAN OCEAN

baobab tree

emu

Aboriginal dancers

WESTERN AUSTRALIA

red kangaroo

dingo

cricket

gold

Perth ●

Australia and Papua New Guinea

Australia is the world's smallest continent. It is a large, wealthy country with a small population. It is hot and dry inland, so most people live in large coastal cities. Australia's wealth comes from farming and mining.

Central Australia is called the "outback." It is mainly deserts and grasslands. Few people live there, but vast numbers of sheep and cattle graze on stations (farms). Australia produces more wool than any other country. It also has large deposits of opals, diamonds, gold, and silver.

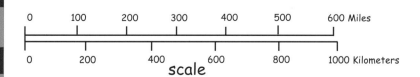

```
0    100   200   300   400   500   600 Miles
```
```
0    200    400    600    800    1000 Kilometers
```
scale

Can you find...

Sydney Opera House?

Ayers Rock (Uluru)?

The Great Barrier Reef is made of coral. It is so big that it can be seen from the Moon.

Darwin

diamonds

salt-water crocodile

cattle

green turtle

meteorite crater

NORTHERN TERRITORY

termite mounds

wallabies

flying doctors

QUEENSLAND

AUSTRALIA

Ayers Rock (Uluru)

grey kangaroos

skyscrapers

Brisbane

koala

opals

Indian-Pacific Railway

SOUTH AUSTRALIA

sheep

Darling R.

pineapple

NEW SOUTH WALES

Sydney Opera House

great white shark

Adelaide

Murrumbidgee R.

Murray R.

Murray R.

Sydney

CANBERRA

grapes

VICTORIA

Melbourne

surfing

GREAT BARRIER REEF

PACIFIC OCEAN

N
W   E
S

Tasmanian devil

TASMANIA

Hobart

Fact:

In Australia, people who live a long way from hospitals depend on the Flying Doctor service when they need medical help. The service allows doctors to travel great distances quickly by airplane.

New Zealand

New Zealand is divided into two islands. Most people live on its volcanic North Island. It has large cattle and sheep ranches and exports lamb and dairy products.

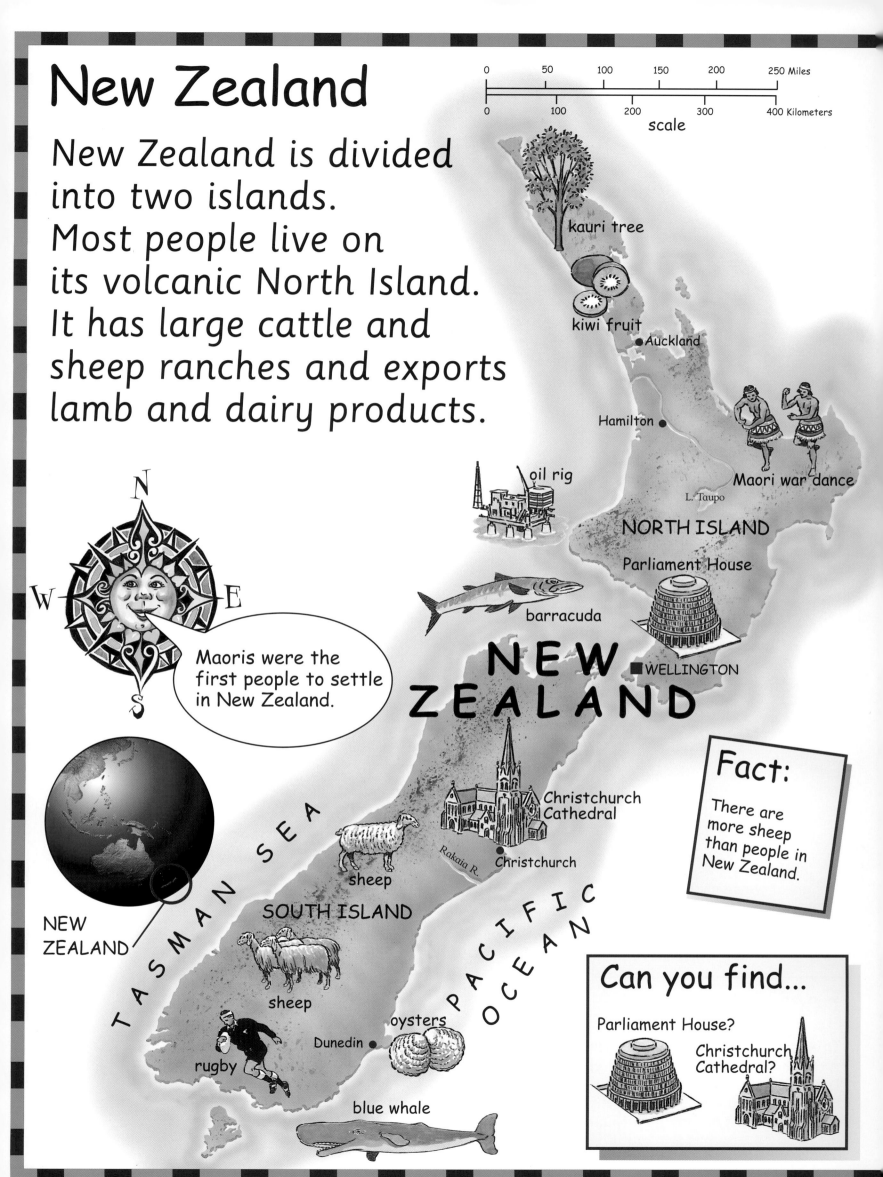

scale

0   50   100   150   200   250 Miles
0   100   200   300   400 Kilometers

kauri tree

kiwi fruit

Auckland

Hamilton

Maori war dance

oil rig

L. Taupo

NORTH ISLAND

Parliament House

barracuda

NEW ZEALAND

■WELLINGTON

Maoris were the first people to settle in New Zealand.

N W E S

NEW ZEALAND

TASMAN SEA

sheep

SOUTH ISLAND

sheep

rugby

Dunedin

oysters

blue whale

PACIFIC OCEAN

Rakaia R.

Christchurch Cathedral

Christchurch

Fact:

There are more sheep than people in New Zealand.

Can you find...

Parliament House?

Christchurch Cathedral?

58

Southwestern Pacific Islands

Thousands of small tropical islands are scattered across the Pacific Ocean east of Australia. Most islanders live in small villages. They fish and grow tropical fruit, including bananas and coconuts.

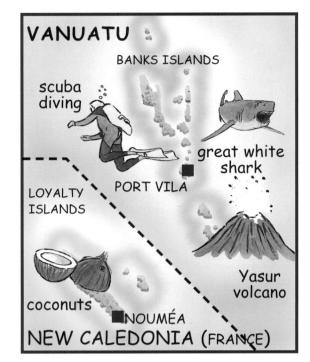

VANUATU

BANKS ISLANDS

scuba diving

great white shark

LOYALTY ISLANDS

PORT VILA

Yasur volcano

coconuts

■NOUMÉA

NEW CALEDONIA (FRANCE)

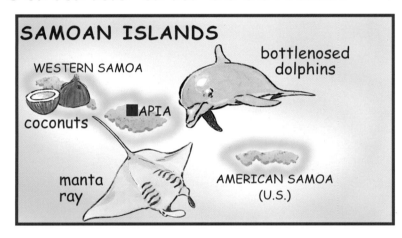

SAMOAN ISLANDS

WESTERN SAMOA

bottlenosed dolphins

coconuts

■APIA

manta ray

AMERICAN SAMOA (U.S.)

BOUGAINVILLE

house on stilts

NEW GEORGIA ISLANDS

■HONIARA bananas

SANTA CRUZ ISLANDS

SOLOMON ISLANDS

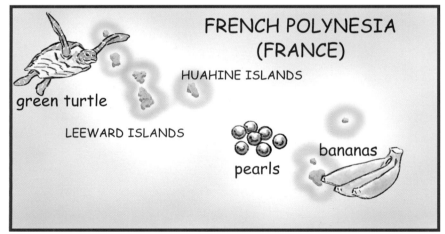

FRENCH POLYNESIA (FRANCE)

HUAHINE ISLANDS

green turtle

LEEWARD ISLANDS

pearls

bananas

Fact:

The people of Bougainville in the Solomon Islands have discovered how to use coconut oil as a fuel for cars.

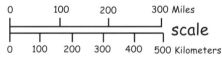

scale

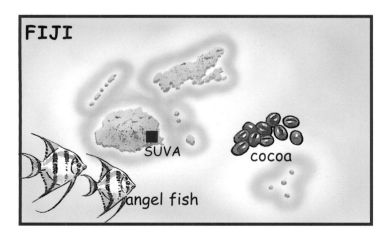

FIJI

SUVA

cocoa

angel fish

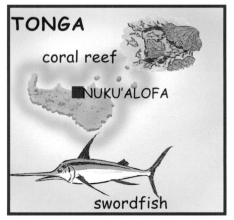

TONGA

coral reef

■NUKU'ALOFA

swordfish

SOUTHWESTERN PACIFIC ISLANDS

The Arctic

The Arctic Ocean is covered in thick ice at the North Pole. The Inuit and Sami are the only people who live in this harsh environment, but many animals and plants survive there.

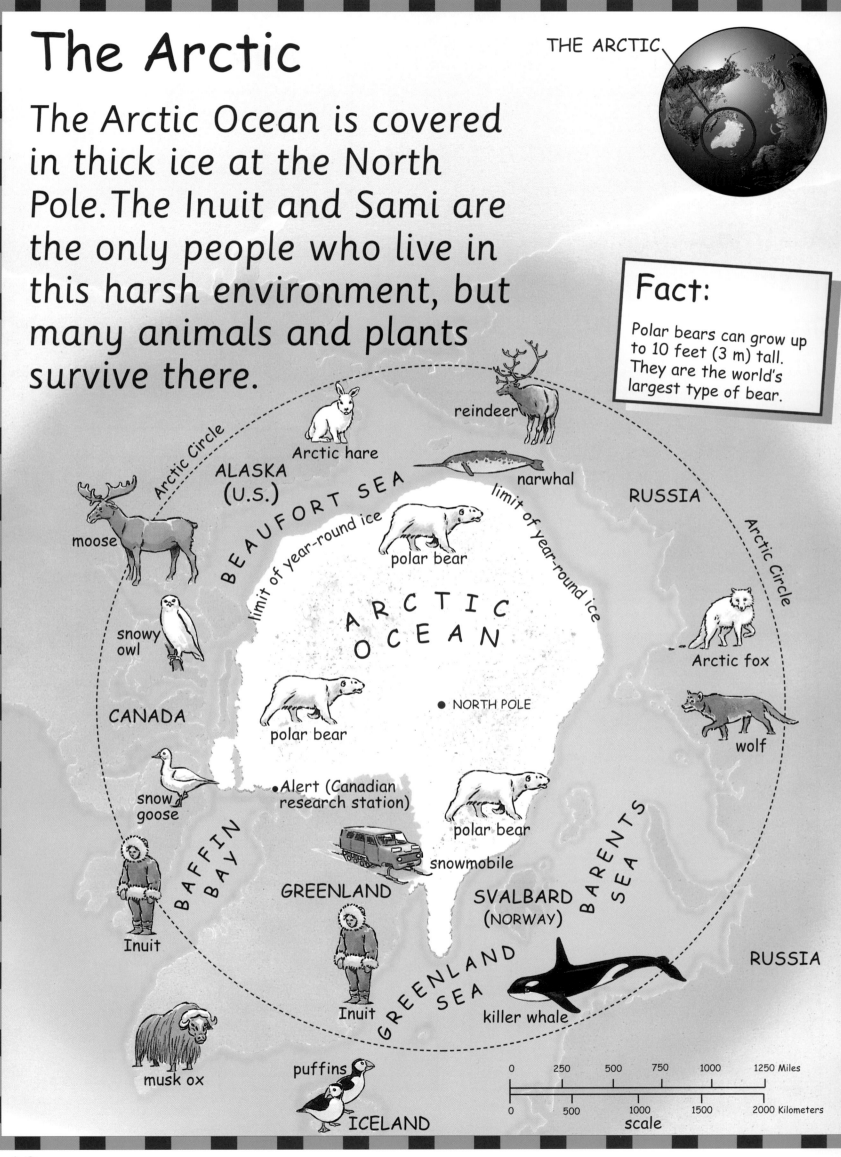

THE ARCTIC

Fact:
Polar bears can grow up to 10 feet (3 m) tall. They are the world's largest type of bear.

Arctic Circle

ALASKA (U.S.)

Arctic hare

reindeer

narwhal

RUSSIA

BEAUFORT SEA

limit of year-round ice

limit of year-round ice

Arctic Circle

moose

polar bear

ARCTIC OCEAN

snowy owl

Arctic fox

CANADA

polar bear

NORTH POLE

wolf

snow goose

Alert (Canadian research station)

polar bear

BAFFIN BAY

BARENTS SEA

Inuit

GREENLAND

snowmobile

SVALBARD (NORWAY)

RUSSIA

GREENLAND SEA

Inuit

killer whale

musk ox

puffins

0   250   500   750   1000   1250 Miles

0   500   1000   1500   2000 Kilometers

scale

ICELAND

The Antarctic

The South Pole in the Antarctic is the coldest place on Earth. No country owns this frozen continent, but many have set up scientific research stations there.

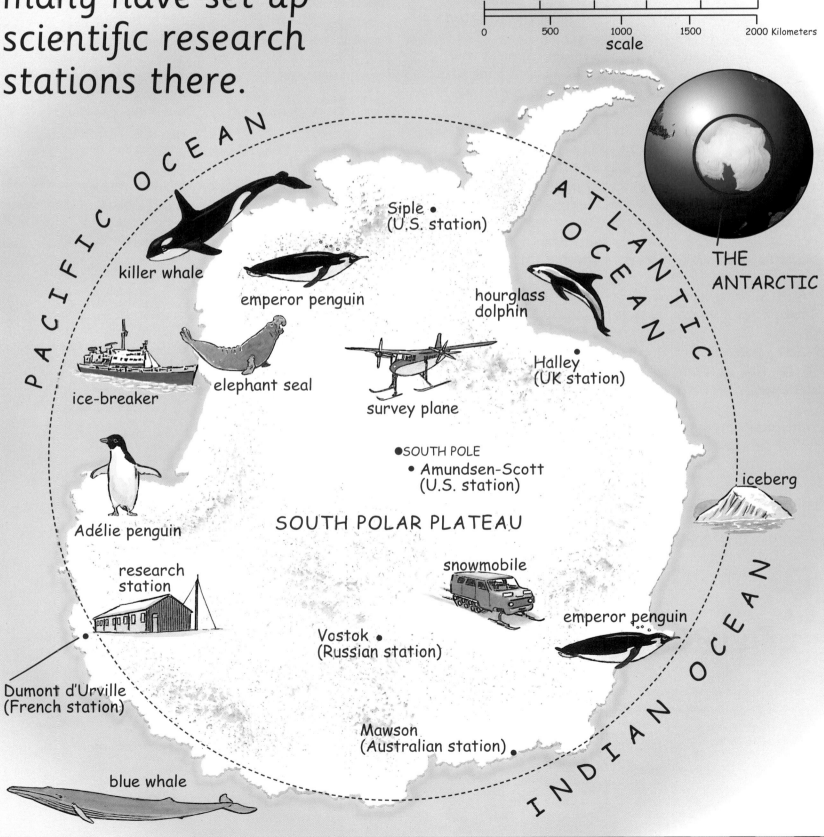

0   250   500   750   1000   1250 Miles

0   500   1000   1500   2000 Kilometers

scale

THE ANTARCTIC

PACIFIC OCEAN

ATLANTIC OCEAN

INDIAN OCEAN

Siple (U.S. station)

killer whale

emperor penguin

hourglass dolphin

elephant seal

ice-breaker

survey plane

Halley (UK station)

●SOUTH POLE

● Amundsen-Scott (U.S. station)

SOUTH POLAR PLATEAU

iceberg

Adélie penguin

research station

snowmobile

emperor penguin

Dumont d'Urville (French station)

Vostok (Russian station)

Mawson (Australian station)

blue whale

Glossary

climate The average weather of a region.

continent One of the large masses of land on the Earth's surface.

desert An area that has very little or no rainfall.

equator The imaginary line around the center of the Earth. The areas around the equator are the parts of the planet closest to the Sun.

export Something that is sent from one country to be sold in another.

fertile Soil that will grow plenty of crops.

humid Warm and damp.

hurricane A storm with very strong winds.

independence Freedom from rule by another country.

latitude Imaginary lines that run horizontally around the Earth.

longitude Imaginary lines that run vertically around the Earth.

map projection The process of forming a flat map by "stretching" a globe.

monsoon A strong wind that usually also brings heavy rain.

northern hemisphere The half of the Earth north of the equator.

peninsula A narrow area of land that sticks out far into the sea.

permanent Long-lasting.

population The number of people who live in a place.

southern hemisphere The half of the Earth south of the equator.

summit The highest point of a mountain.

tropical Very warm and humid, as in the areas around the equator.

volcanic Formed by a volcano.

Index

A
Abu Dhabi (United Arab Emirates) 43
Abuja (Nigeria) 44
Accra (Ghana) 44
Addis Ababa (Ethiopia) 45
Adelaide (Australia) 57
Adriatic Sea 35, 39
Aegean Sea 36-37
Afghanistan 40, 43, 48
Africa 44-47
Alabama (river) 17
Alabama (state) 17
Alaska (state) 10, 12, 60
Albania 36, 39
Albany (New York) 15
Alberta (Canada) 10
Algeria 44
Algiers (Algeria) 45
Alps, European 29, 33, 35
Alps, Japanese 46
Amazon (river) 20
America
 Central 18-19
 North 10-17
 South 18, 19, 20-21
Amman (Jordan) 42

Amsterdam (Netherlands) 30
Andaman and Nicobar Islands 49
Andaman Sea 52
Andes Mountains 20, 21
Andorra 28, 29
Andorra la Vella (Andorra) 29
Angola 46
Anguilla 19
Ankara (Turkey) 42
Annapolis (Maryland) 15
Antananarivo (Madagascar) 47
Antarctic 61
Antigua and Barbuda 19
Apia (West Samoa) 59
Appalachian Mountains 14, 15
Arabian Sea 43, 48
Arctic 40, 60
Arctic Ocean 10, 41, 60
Argentina 21
Arizona (state) 12-13
Arkansas (river) 16
Arkansas (state) 13, 14, 16-17
Armenia 40, 43
Asmara (Eritrea) 45
Ashgabat (Turkmenistan) 40
Asia 40-43 48-53
Astana (Kazakhstan) 40
Asunción (Paraguay) 21
Athens (Greece) 36, 37
Atlanta (Georgia) 17
Atlantic Ocean 11, 15, 17, 18, 19, 20, 21, 26, 44, 45, 46, 61
Augusta (Maine) 15
Austin (Texas) 16
Australia 53, 56-57, 61
Austria 32-33, 34, 38
Azerbaijan 40, 43

B
Baffin Bay 11, 60
Baffin Island 11
Baghdad (Iraq) 43
Bahamas 19
Bahrain 43
Baku (Azerbaijan) 42
Balearic Islands 27
Baltic Sea 23, 33, 38
Bamako (Mali) 44
Bandar Seri Begawan (Brunei) 53
Bangkok (Thailand) 52
Bangladesh 49
Bangui (Central African Republic) 45
Banjul (Gambia) 44
Barbados 19
Barents Sea 40, 60
Basseterre (St. Kitts and Nevis) 19
Baton Rouge (Louisiana) 17
Bay of Bengal 49
Bay of Biscay 27, 28
Beaufort Sea 60
Beijing (China) 55
Beirut (Lebanon) 42
Belarus 38, 40
Belfast (Northern Ireland) 24
Belgium 29, 30-31, 32
Belgrade (Yugoslavia) 39
Belize 19
Belmopan (Belize) 19
Benin 44
Berlin (Germany) 33
Bern (Switzerland) 32
Bhutan 49, 54, 55
Bishkek (Kyrgyzstan) 40
Bismarck (N. Dakota) 13
Bissau (Guinea-Bissau) 44
Black Sea 39, 40, 42-43
Blue Nile (river) 45
Bogotá (Colombia) 20
Boise (Idaho) 12
Bolivia 21
Borneo 52-53
Bosnia and Herzegovina 38, 39
Boston (Massachusetts) 15
Botswana 47
Brahmaputra (river) 49
Brasília (Brazil) 21
Brazos (river) 16
Bratislava (Slovakia) 38
Brazil 20-21
Brazzaville (Congo Republic) 46
Bridgetown (Barbados) 19

Brisbane (Australia) 57
British Columbia (Canada) 10
British Isles 24-25
British Virgin Islands 19
Brunei 52, 53
Brussels (Belgium) 31
Bucharest (Romania) 39
Budapest (Hungary) 38, 39
Buenos Aires (Argentina) 21
Bujumbura (Burundi) 47
Bulgaria 36, 39, 40, 42
Burkina Faso 44
Burundi 47

C
Cabinda 46
Cairo (Egypt) 45
California (state) 12, 13
Cambodia 52
Cameroon 44, 46
Canada 10-11, 12-13, 14-15, 60
Canary Islands 44
Canberra (Australia) 55
Cape Verde 45
Caracas (Venezuela) 20
Cardiff (Wales) 25
Caribbean 18-19
Caribbean Sea 19
Carson City (Nevada) 12
Caspian Sea 40, 43
Central African Republic 45
Cephalonia 36
Chad 45
Channel Islands 25
Channel Tunnel 24, 25, 29
Charlottetown (Canada) 11
Charleston (West Virginia) 14
Chattahoochee (river) 17
Cheyenne (Wyoming) 13
Chile 21
China 40, 41, 48, 49, 50, 52, 54-55
Chios 36
Colombia 19, 20
Colombo (Sri Lanka) 48
Colorado (river) 12-13, 16
Colorado (state) 13
Columbia (river) 10, 12
Columbia (S. Carolina) 17
Columbus (Ohio) 14
Comoros 47
Conakry (Guinea) 44
Concord (New Hampshire) 15
Connecticut (state) 15
Congo (river) 46, 47
Congo Republic 46
Copenhagen (Denmark) 23
Corfu 36
Corsica 29, 34
Costa Rica 19
Crete 37
Croatia 34, 38, 39
Cuba 19
Cyprus 42
Czech Republic 33, 38, 39

D
Dakar (Senegal) 44
Damascus (Syria) 42
Danube (river) 33, 38, 39
Dar es Salaam (Tanzania) 47
Darling (river) 57
Darwin (Australia) 57
Dead Sea 42
Delaware (state) 15
Democratic Republic of Congo 45, 47
Denmark 10
Denver (Colorado) 13
Des Moines (river) 14
Des Moines (Iowa) 14
Dhaka (Bangladesh) 49
Djibouti (state & capital) 45
Doha (Qatar) 43
Dominica 19
Dominican Republic 19
Don (river) 40
Dover (Delaware) 15
Dublin (Republic of Ireland) 25
Dushanbe (Tajikistan) 40

E
Earth 4-5, 6
East China Sea 50
Ebro (river) 27
Ecuador 20
Edinburgh (Scotland) 24
Edmonton (Canada) 10
Egypt 42, 44, 45
El Salvador 19
Elbe (river) 33
England 24, 25
English Channel 25, 28
Equatorial Guinea 46
Eritrea 45
Estonia 40
Ethiopia 45, 47
Euphrates (river) 43
Eurasia 40-41
Europe 22-39, 40
Everglades 17

F
Falkland Islands 21
Fiji 59
Finland 22-23, 40
Flint (river) 17
Florida (state) 17
Fort-de-France (Martinique) 19
France 15, 25, 27, 28-29, 31, 32, 34, 61
Frankfort (Kentucky) 14
Fredericton (Canada) 11
Freetown (Sierra Leone) 44
French Guiana 20
French Polynesia 59

G
Gabon 44, 46
Gaborone (Botswana) 47
Galapagos Islands 20
Gambia 44
Ganges (river) 48, 49
Garonne (river) 28
Georgetown (Guyana) 20
Georgia 40, 43
Georgia (state) 17
Germany 23, 29, 30, 31, 32-33, 38
Ghana 44
Gibraltar 26
Godavari (river) 48
Great Barrier Reef 57
Great Lakes 14, 15
Greece 36-37, 39, 42
Greenland 10-11, 60
Greenland Sea 60
Grenada 19
Guadeloupe 19
Guatemala 19
Guatemala City (Guatemala) 19
Guinea 44
Guinea-Bissau 44
Gulf of Bothnia 22-23
Gulf of Mexico 16, 17, 18, 19
Guyana 20

H
Hainan 55
Haiti 19
Halifax (Canada) 11
Hanoi (Vietnam) 52
Harare (Zimbabwe) 47
Harrisburg (Pennsylvania) 15
Hartford (Connecticut) 15
Havana (Cuba) 19
Hawaii (state) 12, 13
Helena (Montana) 13
Helsinki (Finland) 23
Himalayas 48, 49, 54
Hobart (Australia) 57
Honduras 19
Honiara (Solomon Islands) 59
Honolulu (Hawaii) 13
Hudson Bay 11
Hungary 33, 38, 39, 40

I
Iberian Peninsula 26
Iceland 22, 60
Idaho (state) 12-13
Ijssel (river) 30
Ikaria 36

Illinois (state) 14
India 48-49, 54, 55
Indian Ocean 45, 47, 48, 49, 52, 56, 61
Indiana (state) 14
Indianapolis (Indiana) 14
Indonesia 52-53
Indus (river) 48, 49
Ionian Sea 36
Iowa (state) 13, 14
Iran 40, 43, 48
Iraq 42-43
Ireland, Republic of 24-25
Irian Jaya 53
Irish Sea 25
Irrawaddy (river) 49
Islamabad (Pakistan) 48
Israel 42, 45
Italy 29, 33, 34-35, 39
Ivory Coast 44

J
Jackson (Mississippi) 17
Jakarta (Indonesia) 52
Jamaica 19
Japan 50-51
Java 52-53
Jefferson City (Missouri) 14
Jerusalem (Israel) 42, 43
Jordan 42, 45
Juneau (Alaska) 12

K
Kabul (Afghanistan) 48
Kampala (Uganda) 47
Kansas (state) 13, 14
Kathmandu (Nepal) 48
Kazakhstan 40, 41, 54
Kentucky (state) 14, 17
Kenya 45, 47
Kerulen (river) 55
Khartoum (Sudan) 45
Kiev (Ukraine) 40
Kigali (Rwanda) 47
Kingston (Jamaica) 19
Kinshasa (Democratic Republic of Congo) 46
Kos 37
Kosovo 39
Krishna (river) 48
Kuala Lumpur (Malaysia) 52
Kuwait 43
Kuwait City (Kuwait) 43
Kyrgyzstan 40, 54

L
Labrador Sea 11
Lansing (Michigan) 14
Laos 49, 55
La Paz (Bolivia) 21
Latvia 40
Lebanon 42
Lek (river) 30
Lena (river) 41
Lesbos 36
Lesotho 47
Liberia 44
Libya 44
Liechtenstein 33
Ligurian Sea 34
Lilongwe (Malawi) 47
Lima (Peru) 20
Limnos 36
Lincoln (Nebraska) 13
Lisbon (Portugal) 26
Lithuania 38, 40
Little Rock (Arkansas) 16
Ljubljana (Slovenia) 39
Loire (river) 28
Lomé (Togo) 44
London (United Kingdom) 24, 25
Louisiana (state) 17
Low Countries 30-31
Lower Tunguska (river) 41
Luanda (Angola) 46
Lusaka (Zambia) 47
Luxembourg (state & capital) 29, 30-31, 32

M
Maas (river) 31
Macedonia 36, 38, 39
Mackenzie (river) 10
Madagascar 47
Madison (Wisconsin) 14
Madrid (Spain) 27
Main (river) 33
Maine (state) 15
Malabo (Equatorial Guinea) 46
Malawi 47
Malaysia 52, 53
Mali 44
Malta 34, 35
Managua (Nicaragua) 19
Manama (Bahrain) 43
Manila (Philippines) 53
Manitoba (Canada) 11
map-making 6-7
Maputo (Mozambique) 47
Marne (river) 29
Martinique 19
Maryland (state) 14-15
Maseru (Lesotho) 47
Massachusetts (state) 15
Mauritania 44
Mauritius 47
Mbabane (Swaziland) 47
Mediterranean Sea 27, 29, 35, 37, 42, 44-45
Mekong (river) 54-55
Melbourne (Australia) 57
Meuse (river) 31
Mexico 13, 16, 18-19
Mexico City (Mexico) 18
Michigan (state) 14
Middle East 42-43
Mindanao 53
Minnesota (state) 13, 14
Minsk (Belorus) 40
Mississippi (river) 14, 16, 17
Mississippi (state) 17
Missouri (river) 13
Missouri (state) 13, 14, 16-17
Mogadishu (Somalia) 45
Moldova 39, 40
Monaco 28, 29
Mongolia 41, 54-55
Monrovia (Liberia) 44
Montana (state) 12-13
Monte Carlo (Monaco) 29
Montenegro 39
Montevideo (Uruguay) 21
Montgomery (Alabama) 17
Montpelier (Vermont) 15
Montserrat 19
Morocco 26, 44
Moroni (Comoros) 47
Moscow (Russia) 40, 41
Mozambique 47
Murray (river) 57
Murrumbidgee (river) 57
Muscat (Oman) 43
Myanmar 49, 52, 54, 55

N
Nairobi (Kenya) 47
Namibia 46
Narmada (river) 48
Nashville (Tennessee) 17
Nassau (Bahamas) 19
Naxos 37
N'djamena (Chad) 44
Nebraska (state) 13, 14
Nelson (river) 10
Nepal 48-49, 54
Netherlands 30-31, 32
Nevada (state) 12
New Brunswick (Canada) 11
New Caledonia 59
New Delhi (India) 48
New Hampshire (state) 15
New Jersey (state) 15
New Mexico (state) 13, 16
New South Wales (Australia) 57
New York (state) 14-15
New York City 15
New Zealand 58
Newfoundland (Canada) 11
Niagara Falls 11
Niamey (Niger) 44

Nicaragua 19
Nicosia (Cyprus) 42
Niger 44
Niger (river) 44
Nigeria 44
Nile (river) 44, 45
North Carolina (state) 14-15, 17
North Dakota (state) 13, 14
North Korea 54, 55
North Sea 23, 25, 30, 31, 33
Northern Ireland 24, 25
Northern Territory (Australia) 57
Norway 22-23, 60
Norwegian Sea 22
Northwest Territories (Canada) 10
Nouakchott (Mauritania) 44
Nova Scotia (Canada) 11
Nukualofa (Tonga) 59
Nunavut (Canada) 10
Nuuk (Greenland) 11

O
Ohio (river) 14
Ohio (state) 14
Oklahoma (state) 13, 14, 16
Oklahoma City (Oklahoma) 13
Olympia (Washington) 12
Oman 43
Ontario (Canada) 11
Orange (river) 47
Oregon (state) 12
Oslo (Norway) 23
Ottawa (Canada) 11
Ouagadougou (Burkina Faso) 44

P
Pacific Islands, Southwest 59
Pacific Ocean 12, 13, 18, 41, 51, 53, 57, 58, 61
Pakistan 43, 48, 49, 54
Panama 19, 20
Panama Canal 18, 19
Panama City (Panama) 19
Papua New Guinea 53, 56, 57
Paraguay 21
Paramaribo (Suriname) 20
Paris (France) 15, 28
Pearl (river) 17
Pennsylvania (state) 14-15
Persian Gulf 42, 43
Perth (Australia) 56
Peru 20
Philippines 53
Phnom Penh (Cambodia) 52
Phoenix (Arizona) 13
Pierre (S. Dakota) 13
Po (river) 34
Podgorica (Montenegro) 39
Poland 33, 38, 39, 40
Port au Prince (Haiti) 19
Port Louis (Mauritius) 47
Port Moresby (Papua New Guinea) 56
Port of Spain (Trinidad & Tobago) 19
Port Vila (Vanuatu) 59
Porto-Novo (Benin) 44
Portugal 26, 27
Prague (Czech Republic) 38
Praia (Cape Verde) 45
Pretoria (South Africa) 47
Prince Edward Island (Canada) 11
Pristina (Kosovo) 39
Providence (Rhode Island) 15
Puerto Rico 19
Pyongyang (North Korea) 55
Pyrenees Mountains 26, 27, 28-29

Q
Qatar 43
Quebec (Canada) 11
Queensland (Australia) 57
Quito (Ecuador) 20

R
Rabat (Morocco) 44
Rakaia (river) 58
Raleigh (N. Carolina) 17
Red (river) 16-17
Red Sea 42, 45
Regina (Canada) 10
Réunion 47
Reykjavik (Iceland) 22

Rhine (river) 32
Rhode Island (state) 15
Rhodes 37
Rhône (river) 29
Richmond (Virginia) 15
Riga (Latvia) 40
Rio Grande (river) 13, 16
Riyadh (Saudi Arabia) 43
Rocky Mountains 10, 12-13
Romania 39, 40
Rome (Italy) 34
Roseau (Dominica) 19
Russia 23, 38, 40-41, 54-55, 60, 61
Rwanda 47
Ryukyu Islands 50

S
Sacramento (California) 12
Sahara Desert 44
Saint-Denis (Réunion) 47
Salem (Oregon) 12
Salt Lake City (Utah) 12
Sambre (river) 31
Samoan Islands 59
Samos 36
St. George's (Grenada) 19
St. John's (Antigua and Barbuda) 19
St. John's (Canada) 11
St. Kitts and Nevis 19
St. Lucia 19
St. Paul (Minnesota) 14
St. Vincent and the Grenadines 19
San Antonio (river) 16
San José (Costa Rica) 19
San Marino (state & capital) 34
San Salvador (El Salvador) 19
Sana (Yemen) 43
Santa Fe (New Mexico) 13
Santiago (Chile) 21
Santo Domingo (Dominican Republic) 19
Sarajevo (Bosnia and Herzegovina) 39
Sardinia 35
Saskatchewan (Canada) 10-11
Saudi Arabia 42-43, 45
Sava (river) 39
Scandinavia 22-23
Scheldt (river) 31
Scotland 24, 25
Sea of Japan 51
Sea of Okhotsk 41
Seine (river) 28, 29
Selange (river) 55
Senegal 44
Seoul (South Korea) 55
Serbia 39
Severn (river) 25
Seychelles 47
Shannon (river) 25
Shetland Isles 24
Shinano (river) 50-51
Siberia 41

Sicily 35
Sierra Leone 44
Singapore 48
Skiathos 36
Skopje (Macedonia) 39
Skyros 36
Slovakia 33, 38, 40
Slovenia 33, 34, 38
Sofia (Bulgaria) 39
Solomon Islands 59
Somalia 45, 47
South Africa 46-47
South Australia (Australia) 57
South Carolina (state) 17
South China Sea 55
South Dakota (state) 13, 14
South Korea 54, 55
Spain 26-27, 28
Springfield (Illinois) 14
Sri Lanka 48, 49
Stockholm (Sweden) 23
Sudan 45, 47
Sumatra 52
Sun 4, 5
Suriname 20
Swaziland 47
Sweden 22-23
Switzerland 29, 32-33, 34
Sydney (Australia) 57
Syria 42-43

T
Tagus (river) 26
Taipei (Taiwan) 55
Taiwan 54, 55
Tajikistan 40, 48, 54
Tallahassee (Florida) 17
Tallin (Estonia) 40
Tanzania 46, 47
Tapajós (river) 20
Tashkent (Uzbekistan) 40
Tasman Sea 58
Tasmania (Australia) 57
Tbilisi (Georgia) 40
Tegucigalpa (Honduras) 19
Tehran (Iran) 43
Tennessee (state) 14, 17
Texas (state) 13, 16
Thailand 49, 52
Thames (river) 25
Thimpu (Bhutan) 49
Thira 37
Tiber (river) 34
Timor 53
Tirana (Albania) 39
Togo 44
Tokyo (Japan) 50, 51
Tonga 59
Topeka (Kansas) 13
Toronto (Canada) 11
Transylvania 39
Trent (river) 25
Trenton (New Jersey) 15

Trinidad and Tobago 19
Tripoli (Libya) 44
Tunis (Tunisia) 44
Tunisia 44
Turkey 36, 39, 40, 42-43
Turkmenistan 40, 41, 43, 48
Tyrrenhian Sea 35

U
Ucayali (river) 20
Uganda 45, 47
Ukraine 38, 40
Ulan Bator (Mongolia) 55
United Arab Emirates (UAE) 43
United Kingdom (UK) 24-25, 61
United States of America 10, 11, 12-17, 18, 60, 61
Ural Mountains 40, 41
Uruguay 21
Utah (state) 12-13
Uzbekistan 40, 41

V
Vaduz (Liechtenstein) 33
Valletta (Malta) 35
Vanuatu 59
Vatican City 35
Venezuela 20, 21
Vermont (state) 15
Victoria (Australia) 57
Victoria (Canada) 10
Victoria (Seychelles) 47
Victoria Falls 47
Vienna (Austria) 33
Vientiane (Laos) 52
Vietnam 52, 55
Vilnius (Lithuania) 40
Virgin Islands 19
Virginia (state) 14-15, 17

W
Waal (river) 31
Wabash (river) 14
Wales 25
Warsaw (Poland) 38
Washington (state) 12
Washington, D.C. (USA) 15
Wellington (New Zealand) 58
Weser (river) 32
West Bank 42
West Virginia (state) 14-15
Western Australia (Australia) 56-57
Western Sahara 44
Western Samoa 59
White Horse (Canada) 10
White Nile (river) 45
Windhoek (Namibia) 46
Winnipeg (Canada) 11
Wisconsin (state) 14
Wyoming (state) 13

X
Xi (river) 55

Xingu (river) 20
Xizang (Tibet) 54-55

Y
Yamoussoukro (Ivory Coast) 44
Yangon (Myanmar) 49
Yangtze (river) 55
Yaoundé (Cameroon) 44
Yellow (river) 55
Yellowknife (Canada) 10
Yemen 43
Yenisey (river) 40
Yerevan (Armenia) 40
Yugoslavia 38, 39
Yukon Territory (Canada) 10

Z
Zagreb (Croatia) 39
Zaire (river) 47
Zakynthos 36
Zambezi (river) 47
Zambia 47
Zimbabwe 47

Editors:	Karen Barker Smith
	Stephanie Cole
Picture Research:	Nicola Roe
Consultant:	Penny Clarke
Cover design:	Marie O'Neill

Photographic credits

Digital Stock/Corbis Corporation: 20, 25, 32, 35, 37, 41
John Foxx Images: 29, 31, 43, 45
Pictor International: 10, 17, 26, 51
Salariya Book Company: 15

Visit the Salariya Book Company at **www.salariya.com**

Printed on paper from sustainable forests.
Printed and bound in Belgium.

Created, designed and produced by
The Salariya Book Company Ltd
Book House, 25 Marlborough Place,
Brighton BN1 1UB

Published in the United States in 2002 by Franklin Watts,
a Division of Scholastic Inc.
90 Sherman Turnpike, Danbury, CT 06816

A CIP catalog record for this title is available from the
Library of Congress.

ISBN 0-531-14650-2 (Lib. Bdg.)
ISBN 0-531-15587-0 (Pbk.)